SHELDON NATURAL REMEDIES

CIDER VINEGAR

Margaret Hills was born in Co. Kerry, Ireland, in 1925. Moving to England aged 17, she trained as a state registered nurse, married and subsequently became the mother of eight children. She suffered severe arthritis for 16 years, only gaining relief after desperate research led her to start taking apple cider vinegar, among other remedies. Having written four books on arthritis, she now guides others at her clinic in Kenilworth, so that they too can get relief from this very painful condition.

Overcoming Common Problems Series

For a full list of titles please contact
Sheldon Press, Marylebone Road, London NW1 4DU

Overcoming Common Problems Series

Overcoming Common Problems Series

Overcoming Common Problems

SHELDON NATURAL REMEDIES
Cider Vinegar

Margaret Hills SRN

First published in Great Britain in 1997 by
Sheldon Press
SPCK
Marylebone Road
London NW1 4DU

The views expressed in this book are the
author's own and do not in any way
reflect the views of the publisher.

British Library Cataloguing-in-Publication Data
A catalogue record for this book is available from the British Library
ISBN 0–85969–769–X

Photoset by Deltatype Ltd, Birkenhead, Merseyside
Printed and bound by Biddles Ltd, Guildford and King's Lynn

Contents

Preface

I am writing this book in response to the requests of so many of my patients in various parts of the world who are constantly seeking to understand what apple cider vinegar is all about.

Here at the Margaret Hills Clinic great results are being achieved through the use of apple cider vinegar, honey and crude black molasses. These products form the basis of a very effective old-fashioned remedy for ridding the body of the toxic acid which is a root-cause of both osteoarthritis and rheumatoid arthritis. In a previous book, written in 1985 (*Curing Arthritis the Drug-Free Way*), I explained the cause of these diseases. If you would like to learn more about the cause and treatment of your rheumatic condition, detailed information is available in that book, which has helped thousands over the years. *Curing Arthritis – More Ways to a Drug-Free Life*, which followed, gives a lot of information on treatments.

Although most people know of the many benefits of honey and crude black molasses, I have decided to include these products and their benefits in this book. It seems to me that many of my patients are taking these remedies and getting tremendous benefits from using them without actually knowing the reason. I do hope you will find the contents of this book to be of great interest and help.

Margaret Hills

The Margaret Hills Clinic, 1 Oaks Precinct, Caesar Road, Kenilworth, Warwickshire CV8 1DP.

Acknowledgements

My thanks go to my daughter Christine Horner, who has been most helpful in the preparation of this book and who has been involved in the clinic from its very beginning. She is fully qualified to carry on the work of the clinic for years to come.

Also, my special thanks to Margaret Issitt, who wrote the poem *Ignore not the Apple* in praise of cider vinegar.

I would also like to express my appreciation of the help and support provided by my sons, Graham and Bill; also Caroline Peasley, Rachel Uzzell and Caron Roughton whose constant support and encouragement was most valuable.

Introduction

I was introduced to apple cider vinegar in 1960. For the previous 16 years, I had suffered the pain of rheumatoid arthritis. This had worsened gradually until osteoarthritis was diagnosed. I was reduced to a state of continuous pain – sometimes severe, sometimes not so severe – but always there.

It all began in June 1946. I had started to train as a nurse at St Stephen's Hospital in Fulham Road, London, and I enjoyed every moment of it. The ward work was hard but interesting, and the social life was first-class – there was always somebody off-duty to accompany me to the theatre or to the Hammersmith Palais – a favourite dance venue. Free tickets to various London shows were often available to the nurses. In short, we worked hard and we played hard. Life was good, and we enjoyed it.

It had been a particularly busy day on the ward, and as we went to our rooms in the nurses' home we decided we would have a bath and go to the Hammersmith Palais. We had a most enjoyable evening, returning to the hospital ready for a good night's sleep at 11 p.m.

I woke up at about 2 a.m. feeling stiff and in pain. Perhaps I was overtired – I hoped that the feeling would have passed by 7 a.m., when I should be getting up for duty. I had a very restless night. The night sister knocked on my door: 'Time to get up, nurse', she called. I could scarcely move. Every joint was stiff and painful, and I knew I had a high temperature. However, I dragged myself out of bed and on to the ward. The ward sister could see that I was not well. She took my temperature and said: 'My God, girl, you've got rheumatic fever!' She asked a porter to bring a wheelchair to take me to the nurses' sick-bay, and that was the beginning of five long months in bed, on complete rest, not allowed to wash or feed myself, or even to write a letter to my parents.

The rheumatoid virus had attacked my heart. It was very badly enlarged, and my pain, soreness and stiffness are not easily understood by anybody who has not suffered the disease. In the sick-bay I got VIP treatment. Harley Street specialists came every

1

other day to examine my heart. The attention I got from them and my nursing colleagues was second to none.

Having spent five months in bed, I was over the acute stage and was allowed three months convalescence. During my months in hospital, the only treatment I had received was aspirin when the pain became too much, and my sore throat was painted with iodine. Drugs for arthritis had not yet invaded the market – and what a blessing that was.

When my convalescence came to an end, I felt quite good and returned to the hospital to finish my training. That training was to prove invaluable in the clinic I run today, and also in the books I have written on arthritis.

It is important to tell the foregoing story because, without suffering the pain of arthritis at that time and for 16 years afterwards, I would never have been introduced to the apple cider vinegar, honey and crude black molasses, which I have found to be such excellent natural remedies for the many and varied conditions which my patients present me with day after day. I give thanks for the day my next-door neighbour handed me a book written by Dr Jarvis, *Arthritis and Cider Vinegar*. I put his advice into practice and that, coupled with the excellent training I'd had as a nurse, was instrumental in ridding my body of the arthritic pain I had suffered for sixteen years.

Fifteen years ago, I opened a clinic – The Margaret Hills Clinic – for arthritics. Treatment is based on the cider vinegar, honey and molasses regime. The results are extremely satisfying: many patients have got rid of their arthritis and other associated symptoms.

A lot of people today are worried about taking drugs. The shocking truth is that the drugs are harming far too many of us. The side-effects can sometimes be horrendous because many of the drugs used are highly toxic. The informed public know this, and are now turning to natural treatments in a big way. Nothing can be more natural than the three products which are the subject of this book – apple cider vinegar, honey and crude black molasses.

Ignore not the Apple

The poets know, and so do we,
That simple truths will always be
Those that matter to us most;
And so the apple can surely boast
To be at the top of the healing tree.

So reach up high, my friend,
And pluck the fruit I recommend.
It will be pressed, fermented; nothing added
But yeast and time: they'll do their best.
Our native fruit; it gives nectar,
And is known from East to West;
And when the vats are fully emptied,
And bottles, filled, and juice is sold,
The orchards of acetic acid
Transformed into liquid of precious gold,
It is wise to listen, these words to heed:
'Good health is yours'. From a seed
Has grown a tree. Its abundant harvest
Must be to us the very best.

Cider – cyder – there's no difference.
Ignore not the apple, its juice is pure.
As cider vinegar it makes good sense.
Your efforts will bear fruit, I'm sure.

My friend, take heart if you're in pain,
And simply aim for peace again.
Try to smile; not be too low,
And to the health shop quickly go.
Then with your juice please persevere –
And always know – good health is near!

(Margaret Issitt, September 1996)

1

Getting a proper diagnosis

Common problems – such as a headache, back trouble or aches and pains – affect most of us at some point. Usually we know they will clear up by themselves, and we don't want to make a fuss. Sometimes, though, apparently minor symptoms could be the early warning-signs of a more serious disease. It is important not to ignore them because, in many cases, an early diagnosis can make all the difference to successful treatment. However, it is not always easy to tell when a trivial complaint could become more serious. People vary – what is harmless in one case could be serious in another. The main point is to keep an eye open for any change in what is normal for you. Having said that, use your common sense. If in doubt, call the surgery and ask the doctor if your symptoms warrant an immediate appointment.

The following are some of the most common problems that should not be ignored.

1 Unexplained weight-loss

The time of the month (for women), the season, and the amount you eat or exercise, can affect your weight. However, drastic weight-loss can be serious. If your clothes feel loose or people comment on your weight-loss and you have not been dieting, find out why.

Weight-loss – together with thirst, frequent urination, undue tiredness and genital itching – can be a sign of diabetes. It can also indicate an over-active thyroid gland. This problem affects one in ten women, and symptoms include (as well as weight-loss) sweating, inability to relax, weakness, exhaustion, bulging eyes, recurrent diarrhoea, constipation, abdominal pain, nausea or vomiting of blood. Blood in the faeces may mean a digestive tract problem, such as Crohn's disease or a peptic ulcer. If your weight-loss occurs with a loss of appetite and abdominal pain or any change in your bowel habits, then get a proper diagnosis from your doctor.

2 Indigestion

Wind, flatulence, belching, bloating, heartburn, nausea or abdominal pain often occur after eating – in other words, indigestion. This is likely if you have been under stress, eating rich, spicy or fatty foods, or are rushing around after meals. A peptic ulcer can also cause indigestion. In this case you can gain temporary relief by eating something or taking an antacid – but the discomfort will come back. However, indigestion which comes out of the blue, especially if you're over 45, can be a sign of stomach cancer, which is important to catch early. If you regularly have to take antacid drugs, or if your abdominal pain lasts for more than eight hours and you experience loss of appetite or prolonged vomiting, or if there is blood in the vomit or you have dark stools which indicate blood being present, it is very important to make an appointment and get a diagnosis.

3 Sore throat or hoarse voice

Most attacks of sore throat and hoarseness clear up of their own accord. However, if these conditions persist for more than a couple of weeks, investigation by a doctor is necessary. As a rule, the condition is due to smoking or drinking, or an infection due to bronchitis or rhinitis – but the cause could be more sinister, like cancer of the throat. It is very important to get it investigated.

4 Fever

Fever is a sign that the body is fighting infection. Most people's body-temperature is normally 98.6 degrees Fahrenheit (37 degrees centigrade) but elderly people may suffer infections while their temperature stays normal. This is a sign that the body's ability to fight infection has lessened. If the patient has severe shivers, shakes and has chattering teeth (a condition known as a rigor), call a doctor immediately. These can be symptoms of pneumonia, kidney infection or malaria.

Fever, when accompanied by breathlessness, wheezing or blood phlegm, could mean a chest infection. A severe headache, nausea, vomiting, or an aversion to bright lights, stiff neck, breathlessness or abdominal pain – all could be signs of meningitis. Call the doctor without delay. Prompt treatment could mean the difference between life and death.

5 Breathing difficulties

Anything that affects the flow of air into or out of our lungs can cause breathlessness and sometimes pain. Unfit and overweight people become breathless more frequently. Smoking can be a prime cause of breathlessness, and asthma-sufferers, along with those who have allergies to house-dust or animals, can become very breathless. Anaemia, too, can cause breathlessness, as can stress and anxiety. If your breathlessness is accompanied by a cough, high temperature, pain in the chest and weight-loss, it is imperative that you have your doctor's opinion on the cause.

6 Change in bowel habits

Sudden constipation or diarrhoea may be harmless, but could be the result of a digestive disorder such as an irritable bowel. The symptoms of this condition come and go, and there may be many years of respite between bouts. However, in some cases it can persist for months or years, even with treatment. The condition is also known as spastic colon or mucous colitis; it is thought that stress may play a significant role in many cases.

Any change in bowel habits other than diarrhoea could be harmless, and could be due to stress, anxiety, food poisoning or infection. Constipation could be a sign that something else is going wrong. If you notice bright red blood on the toilet paper, you probably have haemorrhoids and, though uncomfortable, these are not serious and can be treated. Blood mixed in with the stools can be a sign of bleeding somewhere along the digestive tract, and needs attention.

On the other hand, a dark bowel-movement may mean that you are taking an iron supplement, or perhaps you have drunk red wine or eaten beetroot. The danger-signs here are a change in your bowel habits that persists for two weeks or more, especially if accompanied by abdominal pain, bleeding or dark faeces. Contact your doctor.

7 Children's ailments

There are no hard-and-fast rules as to when to take your child to the doctor. In babies, breathing difficulties, persistent coughing, vomiting and diarrhoea should all be taken seriously. Children need constant care and watching. A mother can usually tell if her child is off-colour. If it persists, see your doctor. High temperature accompanied by pain, and crying, are good reasons for calling in the doctor.

8 Chest-pain

Chest-pains can be due to all sorts of conditions – not always heart problems as most people think. When the pain is in the front of the chest-wall and worsens on movement, or if you press on it, this can be due to inflammation. The doctor may prescribe an anti-inflammatory drug. Angina causes a crushing pain which usually comes on during exertion and disappears with rest.

Indigestion may be the cause of your chest-pain – that usually comes on after a meal – or you could have been exercising and pulled a muscle. A severe, crushing pain in the centre of the chest could be a heart attack. Chest-pain with breathlessness, if you have had an operation or illness that has kept you in bed, could be an embolism – call your doctor.

9 Vaginal bleeding

Bleeding could be from the uterus, cervix or vagina itself. Causes could include infection, growths like polyps or fibroids, or if you are pregnant, could indicate a miscarriage or placenta problems. Another cause is the contraceptive pill which can cause spotting between periods. You may do better by changing to a different type of pill. Discuss this with your doctor.

Bleeding between your periods or after sex could be a problem. If this occurs, or if there is a blood-stained vaginal discharge after the menopause, see your doctor.

10 Persistent fatigue

Tiredness is usually easy enough to trace back to sleepless nights, overwork, illness, pregnancy or looking after small children. In such cases it is not worth bothering the doctor – though you should make an effort to get more rest.

Persistent fatigue lasting for more than a month may need medical treatment. One common cause is an underactive thyroid, which often develops after the birth of a baby. If your fatigue is accompanied by feelings of cold, hair-loss or thinning of hair, weight-gain or dry skin, it is worth having your thyroid gland checked.

Anaemia is another common cause of fatigue, and is usually accompanied by paleness, faintness, breathlessness and palpitations. Depression too can result in persistent fatigue – other symptoms include weepiness, lack of concentration and interest in life, and a constant low mood. It is imperative that you contact your doctor and find the cause of your problems.

Help your doctor

Your doctor cannot help you if you are not totally honest with him or her. Before visiting the surgery, think over how you have been feeling lately, and whether there has been any significant change in your eating or sleeping habits. Take special note of any other symptoms, even though they may appear to be unrelated to your illness. Keep a diary of when your symptoms occur, how long the problem has lasted, and any possible trigger-factors which you may have noticed.

Try to provide your doctor with as full a picture as possible of your symptoms. For example: do you feel worse at night? What makes you feel better? Can you pinpoint when your symptoms started? If in doubt, get in touch with the surgery beforehand to ask for advice on whether a visit is really necessary.

If your visit is necessary, your doctor will advise you on what to do about your symptoms. That advice could include diet, rest, exercise, physiotherapy or the prescription of a certain drug. On the other hand, the doctor may not be able to diagnose your problems without doing various blood tests. In this case, a blood-sample will be taken and sent to the laboratory for testing. The doctor may decide that you need a barium enema or a barium meal, or maybe X-rays of a particular organ or joint. These are excellent diagnostic aids for the doctor.

Having decided what your problem is, your GP may pass you on to a consultant, who will decide what treatment you should have, and for how long. The consultant will probably need to see you more than once, as an outpatient, to evaluate how you are feeling. Depending on how satisfactory your progress has been, the consultant may discharge you with advice for the future, or may wish to do further investigations.

2

Pure, natural cider vinegar

What is cider vinegar?

Pure, natural cider vinegar must be made from freshly crushed whole apples which have been allowed to ripen or mature, and it should be unpasteurized – do check the label for both these points before you buy. Cider vinegar should be a dark colour and have a heavy pungent odour. It contains powerful enzymes and life-giving minerals: potassium, phosphorus, magnesium, organic sodium, copper, iron, sulphur, chlorine, fluorine, silicon and many other trace minerals – as well as natural malic acid which is so very important in fighting body toxins.

Malt vinegar must not be confused with cider vinegar. Malt vinegar is a refined, processed vinegar which has none of the qualities of natural cider vinegar. Wine vinegars, too, are produced differently and must not be confused with or compared to pure, natural cider vinegar, which is not a mixture of cider and vinegar, as some people think. Taking cider does not have the same beneficial effects on health: cider is a very acidic product, and can be very injurious to a person suffering from rheumatoid arthritis or osteoarthritis – or any disease connected with there being too much acid in the body: migraine, bronchitis, stomach ulcers, Crohn's Disease, diverticulitis, nephritis, cholecystitis or indeed any '-itis'. An '-itis' is an inflammation of a particular organ – often caused by too much toxic acid in the body. Cider adds even more acid, thus adding to the patient's problems. The same applies to malt vinegar: it also is very acidic, and would make any inflammation worse.

Pure, natural cider vinegar can really be called one of nature's more perfect foods. It helps tremendously in reducing overweight. It purifies the cells, ridding the body of poisons. It relieves headaches and migraines, and is wonderful for clearing sore throats (it actually kills the virus which causes them). It fights kidney stones and bladder infections. All these benefits – and many more – can be attributed to the effects of cider vinegar in the body. Day after day, my patients report its many beneficial results. They are amazed – and so am I!

Many doctors don't understand what cider vinegar is, and tell their patients not to take it. This is very sad. In fact, they are building up trouble for their patients in the form of the various diseases which could be avoided or healed with the use of cider vinegar.

Since I opened my clinic in 1982, it has gone from strength to strength: we now treat patients in many countries of the world, the vast majority of whom are helped at a distance, by post! We specialize in arthritis (rheumatoid and osteoarthritis) and the many toxic conditions which are related to an excess of uric acid in the body. The clinic has flourished largely through recommendations. Today's public are educated. They ask questions. They are very worried about the side-effects of drugs, and are turning to natural treatments when they possibly can.

Arthritis is the curse of modern society, reducing people to such a debilitated state that they can't enjoy a productive life. They spend day after day trying to keep pain at bay with the use of the many available drugs: different anti-inflammatories or steroids – all producing various dangerous side-effects, some of which are irreversible.

I give thanks for the day I discovered cider vinegar. I got rid of my arthritis 36 years ago, by taking cider vinegar as part of a good diet containing natural vitamins and minerals, essential for the good health of all.

It is helpful to know precisely what cider vinegar does in your digestive tract, and how and why two teaspoonfuls of cider vinegar in a glass of water at each meal is so good for maintaining bodily health.

This is an example of what happens to bacterial life when cider vinegar is used. Bring a worm in from the garden and put it on a hard surface where you can see it; pour some cider vinegar over it. First it writhes as though in pain; in a few seconds it becomes motionless; then it turns pink, then white, and finally it dies. In the same way, cider vinegar destroys the bacteria in the digestive tract. It closely resembles the gastric juices, normalizes bodily acids and kills off harmful bacteria.

Cider vinegar has very special qualities:

1   It is considered a perfect body-cleanser, acting on the liver and disposing of poisons.
2   It closely resembles the gastric juices and is, therefore, helpful in digestive disorders.
3   It contains many valuable vitamins and trace elements.
4   Because it improves metabolism, it deals with excess fat in the body.
5   It aids digestion and absorption.
6   It relieves laryngitis, coughs, asthma and sore throats if used as a gargle.
7   It is invaluable in arthritis and rheumatic complaints.
8   Liver and kidney troubles (e.g. cystitis) also respond to it.

The humble apple

People have eaten apples for thousands of years. The saying, 'An apple a day keeps the doctor away', is very familiar. The apple is one of God's great foods. It is one of the richest sources of potassium – a mineral which has a wonderful effect on the arteries, keeping them flexible and resilient. A lot of older people today suffer from hardening of the arteries. This can be a very painful condition which robs the sufferer of the benefits and joys of later years. Potassium also fights dangerous bacteria and viruses – it is indeed a powerful mineral that is found in the humble apple.

Potassium deficiency can be a problem for older people, a lot of whom consume vast amounts of salt and eat very little of the potassium-rich vegetables and fruits, particularly apples. Due to denture-problems they do not eat apple-skins or potato-skins, both of which are rich in potassium and older people, as a rule, do not get much exercise and sit for long periods of time. This contributes to oedema of the tissues (particularly in the legs); high cholesterol and hardening of the arteries.

Figure 1 shows that the apple is a wonderful source of nutrition, especially of potassium. Apples also contain a surprisingly low amount of sugar – just 8 per cent, and this in a readily digestible form. Apples can be eaten raw. There is a tremendous supply available, and there is no difficulty in finding a great

Figure 1 Analysis of an apple.

calories	81.4 kcal	% calories from fat	5%
total fat	0.5 g	% calories from carbohydrates	93.8%
saturated fat	0.1 g	% calories from protein	1.2%
monounsaturated fat	0 g	% refuse	8%
polyunsaturated fat	0.1 g	vitamin C	8 mg
cholesterol	0 mg	vitamin A	73 iu
carbohydrate	21.1 g	vitamin B6	0.07 mg
dietary fibre	3.7 g	vitamin B12	0 mcg
protein	0.3 g	thiamine B1	0.02 mg
sodium	0 mg	riboflavin B2	0.02 mg
potassium	159 mg	folacin	3.9 mcg
calcium	10 mg	niacin	0.1 mg
iron	0.3 mg	caffeine	0 mg
zinc	0.1 mg	alcohol	0 g

variety because of the amount imported from other countries. There is nothing to touch an organically grown apple, and pure, natural cider vinegar which is derived from fermented, organically grown, apples is a first-class, God-given product for the relief of so many conditions.

There is a tremendous lack of confidence in drugs these days. Patients come to our clinic full of fear about the current state of their health, the uncertainty of improvement brought about by taking recognized drugs for arthritis; fear of side-effects from those drugs, and fear for the future. Many are told, 'Learn to live with it' – but it can be excruciatingly painful, and that in itself is frightening when nothing seems to relieve it. People worry about losing their mobility and also their independence.

Even young people feel constantly tired – their get-up-and-go has got up and gone. They feel half-sick most of the time. Their vitamin and mineral deficiency is very evident. They look tired, run-down and lifeless. Their skin and muscle tone is bad, particularly the skin over the eyes which prolapses, so that the eyes look like slits instead of being wide open. All of this can be due to a lack of potassium in the diet, or may be due to the side-effects of drugs.

Symptoms of potassium deficiency

1 Irritability and impatience.
2 Sometimes a cold feeling all over, especially cold hands and cold feet.
3 Physical and mental tiredness.
4 Loss of memory and forgetfulness.
5 Aching bones and muscles.
6 Lower back-pain.
7 Itching eyes, sometimes bloodshot and watery.
8 Mental fatigue.
9 Depression and nervousness.
10 Itchy scalp, dandruff and, sometimes, premature balding.

Cider vinegar and oedema

Many people come to the clinic because they have arthritis, have been on drugs for years and are getting worse. Apart from arthritis, a lot of them have hardening of the arteries, angina, high blood pressure and oedema. They tell us that they are taking drugs for these conditions (e.g. water-tablets for the oedema). The water-tablets get rid of the oedema, but in so doing drain the body of vital vitamins and minerals, especially potassium. General fluid-retention may result in swelling of the fingers (causing rings to feel tight), and puffiness of the face and upper and lower eyelids. Our treatment for this condition consists of taking cider vinegar – two dessertspoons well dissolved in plenty of water, three times daily. Also it is important to cut out salt from the diet (salt retains water in the body), and to cut out refined carbohydrates such as sugar, white bread, cakes and glucose drinks, cola and so on. Food allergies produce fluid-retention: wheat and other grains, as well as milk, can have this effect on some people. It is important to find out if any of these is the cause of the fluid retention and, if so, to cut them out of the diet. If fluid-retention persists, the cause should be investigated and a true diagnosis obtained. Invariably, when the patient adheres to the above programme (coupled with the vitamins and minerals advised by us for their particular condition), great results are obtained. Overweight patients lose their excess weight, and become happy, positive people. We have found that prescribing cider vinegar for our oedema patients has been very successful. Cider vinegar is a powerful diuretic: while getting rid of excess body-fluids through the kidneys, it also supplies potassium and other minerals to the body.

It must be understood that cider vinegar alone will not reduce oedema or overweight without a conscious effort on the patient's part to control the excess intake of food and of sugary and alcoholic drinks.

Exercise too, is very important – a gradual build-up is desirable. The overweight patient with excess body-fluid will not be very keen to exercise, but making an effort each day will bring visible results and be an encouragement to do more.

The diet should consist of raw salads if possible, fruit as prescribed (e.g. arthritics should not have citrus fruits) and plenty of green vegetables such as cabbage, runner beans, spinach and celery, as well as lean lamb, plenty of white fish, cottage cheese and skimmed milk. No hard cheese and no beef or pork should be eaten. These meats contain a lot of uric acid, especially meat from animals which have been factory farmed. When such meat is eaten, a large amount of residual poisons is taken into the system, because the animal-feed has been laced with chemicals (antibiotics, steroids, hormones, etc).

Cider vinegar for sore throats

I have brought up a family of eight children, five boys and three girls. I have had to combat many and varied conditions – childhood illnesses, coughs, colds, sore throats, bronchial problems, kidney problems, etc., including my own rheumatoid and osteoarthritis. I married at 25 and my first child was born when I was 27 years old. My son, Michael, was born with a twisted bowel. Thirteen months later, Christine was born – she had a similar problem. In those days, I relied heavily on the medical profession – and I must say that treatment was excellent. Both children have grown up strong, healthy and intelligent – as indeed have all the others.

In those days, cider vinegar was unheard of – there was only one sort of vinegar. There was a mother plant in the bottle ('mother' being the term used to describe the scum which forms on top of the cider when alcohol turns to vinegar, i.e. during fermentation). Vinegar was then a very dark colour and it was used in all sorts of conditions. Today, cider vinegar is nowhere near as strong or as dark-looking, but nevertheless it has wonderful effects in the treatment of various illnesses, not least of sore throats.

At the first sign of a sore throat, I reach for the cider vinegar. I put two tablespoons of cider vinegar in a cup or glass, and fill it with cold water. I gargle with that three or four times a day, and drink the same cocoction throughout the day and night. My sore throat does not last for very long. For those who do not gargle (i.e. young children), take a piece of lint folded to fit around the child's neck, plunge it into about 200 ml/a third of a pint of warm water to which two tablespoons of cider vinegar have been added; squeeze it out and apply to the throat and neck at night. Cover this with cotton-wool and a crepe bandage. The cider vinegar draws out the toxins as the child sleeps. I have always used this on my family, and now my daughters are grown-up, they carry on the tradition in their families. They know the value of cider vinegar.

Viral and bacterial infections are responsible for colds, tonsillitis, laryngitis, adenoids and quinsy. Sometimes, during an attack of tonsillitis, an abscess forms behind a tonsil. The affected side of the throat becomes very painful, and the infection may spread to the ear. This is a very painful condition known as quinsy. There is also difficulty in swallowing and speaking. For all these conditions, the patient should drink plenty of fluids, particularly water with two teaspoons of cider vinegar added. The cider vinegar compress mentioned above should help to draw out the toxins.

Vitamin C and zinc tablets are excellent for strengthening the immune system and thereby fighting the infection which is causing the sore throat. However, a sore throat can make swallowing difficult – so when tablets cannot be swallowed whole, crush them. Vitamin C – at least 500mg three times daily – should be taken, and zinc should be a great help to the immune system. Ordinary sore throats can usually be dealt with at home, but with a quinsy it is wise to contact your GP, because of the possible spread of infection to the ear. The doctor may decide to give an antibiotic to clear the infection and release the pus from the abscess. Whatever the doctor's decision, the cider-vinegar gargle, drink and compress can be invaluable. Some people prefer to take their cider-vinegar drink with honey to sweeten it.

Cider vinegar drink

Add one to two teaspoons of clear honey to approximately half a pint or less (300 ml) of warm (not boiling) water. Add one dessertspoon of cider vinegar, and drink or sip. (If boiling water is added, it could destroy some of the minerals in the cider vinegar.) This is an excellent drink. The honey is a natural health-giving, energy-giving product, and the cider vinegar has got the power to kill the germs or viruses that are the cause of the problem.

Cider vinegar for overweight

First and foremost, to reduce weight it is important to regulate food-intake. It is also important to remember that overweight can be due to many factors: lack of exercise, emotional problems, fluid-retention as a result of drug-taking for various conditions. If the cause of overweight can be diagnosed and removed, a natural weight-reduction can be achieved quite quickly, with a sensible diet and cider vinegar.

Approximately one third of the whole population are overweight, and those who are have an increased chance of developing any of the following ailments: high blood pressure, heart disease, gall bladder problems, osteoarthritis, gout, diabetes, circulatory problems, oedema. Diet plays a big part in the reduction of weight. The acid-free diet which we advise for both osteoarthritis and rheumatoid arthritis achieves wonderful results, along with the use of cider vinegar.

The acid-free diet consists of cutting out lactic acid, which is found in butter, hard and soft cheese, fresh milk and cream. We ask our patients to use skimmed milk when necessary, cottage cheese instead of the other cheeses, very low-fat vegetable margarine instead of butter, and no cream or red meats (beef or pork and their derivatives). Wholemeal bread is much better than white bread. If the patient is very overweight, we advise two dessertspoons of cider vinegar in a glass of cold or hot (not boiled) water three times daily. The cider vinegar is a powerful diuretic, which drains the body of excessive fluid. The patient must expect frequent visits to the toilet to urinate. This cider vinegar and diet treatment works extremely well, for example, for the relief of bakers' cysts which can be so uncomfortable at the back of the knee, and daily exercise is very beneficial if possible.

Cider vinegar for the prostate gland

George used my cider vinegar and an acid-free diet to get rid of his arthritis. I was amazed when he wrote to tell me that, not only had it got rid of his arthritis but it had also shrunk his prostate gland which had been giving him so much trouble that he was expecting to have an operation. Now he does not need it. His doctor, too, was amazed.

Cider vinegar for arthritis

At my natural health clinic, we treat patients suffering from both osteoarthritis and rheumatoid arthritis. People visit the clinic for personal consultation, and we have devised a postal treatment for those who live too far away. Our patients often ask: 'Will cider vinegar cure my arthritis?' I have to reply: 'I don't believe in "cures". In my opinion, the body cures itself, if given the right conditions.' The body is a powerful mechanism which heals itself when treated properly.

This conviction is based on my personal experience. I have already described my experience of rheumatic fever, after recovering from which, I was able to finish my nurse-training and marry. But after my first child was born, the arthritis reappeared and gradually through the years got worse until eventually I had both osteoarthritis and flare-ups of rheumatoid arthritis. Life was pretty hard in those days: no washing machines, no vacuum cleaners, all nappy-washing was by hand, and I was always in pain. The years passed. We had six healthy children who needed a lot of attention. I'm sure that the stress of being unable to look after my family properly contributed to the awful flare-up of rheumatoid arthritis which confined me to a wheelchair, in constant pain, practically unable to move. The medical profession did their best, giving me a drug called phenylbutazone and telling me that I would have to learn to live with it. The drug causes hardening of the liver, so I was advised to take as little as possible.

It was at that time that my neighbour handed me a book by Dr Jarvis, a medical man in Vermont. He extolled the virtues of cider vinegar in the treatment of arthritis. I began to follow his recommendations, and combining them with an acid-removing diet, vitamins and minerals, I got rid of my arthritis. I have never looked back. I was then 37 years old. I am now 71, and for the past 34 years arthritis has not bothered me.

We have to fight the acid crystals which build up in our bodies all our lives. Pure cider vinegar dissolves these crystals and passes them out naturally through the kidneys. When these acids accumulate in the joints, the patient suffers from osteoarthritis. Excruciating pain is experienced on movement and there is a wearing-away of the synovial membranes which cover the joints. This results in a crunching and creaking of the joints – a condition called crepitus. There is widespread deformity of the finger-joints, also the wrists, knees and feet. One of my patients had very badly deformed fingers – but having spent eighteen months on the cider-vinegar treatment, she now has beautifully straight fingers and pain-free hands. I have the 'before and after' photographs she sent me. She is only one of the many happy patients who have had amazing results. Acid crystals affect the muscles, especially the muscles at the front of the arm. Many patients cannot lift their arms to shoulder-level without extreme pain. The muscles become weak, flabby and powerless.

Rheumatoid arthritis is caused by a streptococcal infection. As a rule, it starts with flu-like symptoms, i.e. sore throat, headache, shivering, high temperature, etc. Cider vinegar can play a large part in the treatment of this condition: in my opinion, if the patient's body is not full of acid, the streptococcus cannot survive and he/she will not succumb to rheumatoid arthritis. The cider vinegar gets brilliant results with both rheumatoid and osteoarthritis – which makes me believe that acid crystals are the primary cause of both diseases. The number of happy, arthritis-free patients who have passed through our hands in the past 14 years shows what our treatment can do – and the basis of that treatment is apple cider vinegar.

Cider vinegar is an integral part of natural treatment for the relief of any form of arthritis. However, because the acid crystals have generally been building up for a long time in order to have resulted in arthritis, other health problems may also be present.

These may include such complaints as ulcers, hiatus hernia, diabetes, etc. It is necessary to state, therefore, that the quantity of cider vinegar to be taken varies, depending on the individual.

Start with a small quantity – for example, one teaspoon of cider vinegar with one teaspoon of honey (to be omitted in the case of diabetes) in a large glass of water, taken once daily. Once you are comfortable with this quantity, increase to two, and then three drinks daily. Having settled into that routine, gradually increase the amount of cider vinegar in each drink until you are taking one dessertspoon of cider vinegar with one teaspoon of honey in a large glass of water, three times daily.

Diet too is very important, and an acid-free diet should be maintained. Where arthritis is concerned, it is also imperative to take supplementary nutrition – i.e. vitamins, minerals and protein – to compensate for foods omitted in the diet, and to strengthen the ability to eliminate the acid crystals.

Cider vinegar for headaches

Almost everybody has headaches at some time. Most headaches are caused by tension in the muscles of the scalp and neck after periods of concentration or stress. Some result from eating problems, food-allergies, or alcohol abuse – the familiar hangover. Some are connected with the cold or flu virus. If a person suffers from sinus problems, these are usually accompanied by a very unpleasant headache. Measles and meningitis produce a headache which is aggravated by bright lights. Brain tumours can also cause headaches, as can a knock on the head – internal bleeding may be the cause. If headaches occur frequently or persist for a long time, a doctor's opinion should be sought.

Migraine is a type of very severe headache. 'Migraine' means 'half of the head', and is usually confined to one side of the head only, sometimes involving numbness or weakness down one side of the face or body. This is all due to the involvement of the nervous system. Migraines can be inherited, and usually affect people with good intelligence and considerable energy. These people are usually sensitive and sympathetic; they can be fussy, demanding, ambitious and sometimes aggressive. Usually, with the classic migraine, the sufferer gets spots or flashes of lights before the eyes, and often feels nauseous. Sometimes fears or emotions can trigger a migraine. Schoolchildren can be very prone to migraines but as they grow older, attacks may get less frequent and diminish altogether.

The daily intake of apple cider vinegar helps to correct and maintain the body's acid-alkaline balance. Two teaspoons, three times daily, in a glass of water, is very often sufficient to ward off an attack; this should be taken every day regardless, with an extra dose if a headache or migraine occurs.

Another way to use apple cider vinegar in the treatment of headaches or migraines is the vaporizing method: equal quantities of cider vinegar and water are heated together, either in a saucepan on the stove or in a microwave. When fumes begin to rise from the liquid, remove the pan from the heat, set it down on a table and lean the head over to inhale the vapours until you find that the headache subsides. This is a much better treatment than headache tablets which often produce various side-effects.

Cider vinegar for high blood pressure

Taking your blood pressure is the only means of finding out how hard your heart has to work to pump blood through your body. Blood pressure fluctuates from time to time, depending on what you are doing, mentally or physically (e.g. whether you are resting, eating, or are in a state of nervous stress and strain) – although the brain has to receive one-and-a-half pints of blood every minute. Blood pressure also varies according to the weather: it seems to be highest in cold weather and lowest in warm weather.

High blood pressure is called hypertension and low blood pressure is called hypotension. It is generally accepted that the highest appropriate reading is 100 plus your age, over 90. For instance, a 70-year-old with a reading of 170/90 is not considered to need treatment.

Hypotension (abnormally low blood pressure) is, in my opinion, just as bad as high blood pressure. The heart is not performing as it should be, and usually the patient is either anaemic or has a malfunctioning thyroid. When I find a patient with very low blood pressure I ask the patient's doctor to test for anaemia and/or a thyroid problem.

Stress is a very common factor in the development of high blood pressure, but the following can all have a devastating effect on the blood pressure.

- eating too much salt;
- taking too little exercise;
- drinking too much alcohol;
- taking the contraceptive pill;
- smoking;
- taking steroids and other drugs for arthritis;
- kidney disorders;
- HRT (hormone replacement therapy), which sometimes causes weight-gain and raises the blood pressure;
- hardening of the arteries (in older women and men).

Men and women with responsible positions at work sometimes have high blood pressure due to the nature of the job and their responsibility for others. The number of such sufferers is rapidly increasing. High blood pressure is an associated factor in deaths due to heart and kidney disease.

The heart is the hardest-working muscle in the whole of the body, so it must have a constant supply of power and energy to enable it to continue beating night and day. It is very difficult to determine whether high blood pressure is a symptom of a disease, or a disease in itself.

The first blood pressure reading taken at my clinic is apt also to be the highest, because of the patient's apprehension and anxiety – sometimes we take it again before the patient leaves, only to find that it has returned to normal as the tension has disappeared.

The treatment for high blood pressure should consist of a diet rich in fresh salads and carbohydrates. Eating protein is quite in order, if it is offset by an increased acid intake such as cider vinegar, apples, grapes, cranberries or their juices. The blood is always alkaline, but its alkalinity can be increased or decreased. Increased alkalinity thickens the blood, which sometimes results in an increase in blood pressure. Therefore it is most important to balance our intake of protein (which is alkaline) with an acid drink – and there is nothing to touch a glass of water with two teaspoons of cider vinegar, two or three times daily.

Cider vinegar gives to the heart that powerful mineral potassium, which strengthens the heart muscle. Potassium dissolves the body-acids thereby preventing the blood from thickening. Many drugs, including the contraceptive pill, raise the blood pressure; smoking narrows the arteries which again contributes to high blood pressure – the pill and smoking should be avoided. Restricting the intake of alcohol, losing weight, and taking regular gentle exercise are all important in maintaining healthy blood pressure.

Cider vinegar for kidney stones

Most people are born with two kidneys which filter waste products from the blood into the urine. The urine then passes to the bladder and from there, out of the system. The kidneys are two very important organs which play a vital part in maintaining the body's fluid balance.

Various disorders can affect the kidneys, the most common being kidney stones which usually contain uric acid and calcium. When the stones are in the kidneys they cause no pain, but when they become dislodged and start to travel down the urinary tract, the pain they can cause is second-to-none. Sometimes stones block the urinary tract, causing severe back-pain in the kidney region, and spreading round to the abdomen and into the groin. Very often the patient gets pain on passing urine, and blood may be present in the urine.

Most kidney stones can be dissolved with cider vinegar, which is excellent in combating uric acid. I would suggest one dessertspoon of cider vinegar in a glass of cold water daily, with or without one teaspoon of honey. Cider vinegar should be used freely on all green salads; it is also important to eat beetroot, parsley, celery, cucumber, carrots and green onions, which are all wonderful body cleansers. Nettle tea, too, is a great cleanser. Bladder and kidney infections may also be treated in the same way.

Cider vinegar for cramps

Cramps are muscular spasms. They usually affect the legs, feet, toes and fingers. Whenever it occurs, it is an excruciating pain at the time – and leaves residual pain in the muscle, sometimes for days afterwards. Typists, gardeners and athletes are very prone to cramp in the muscles which get repeatedly used; people who do a lot of writing can get writer's cramp.

I worked in factory surgeries for some time and, especially in the hot weather, men would come to the surgery with severe cramp. Because of the heat in the foundries, it was nearly always caused by a lack of salt – because of the salt lost through sweating. If a man came to the surgery frequently with cramps we would suspect a more serious cause, and have him checked out by the factory doctor – because cramps can have many causes, e.g. circulation problems, or a lack of calcium or other minerals. A lot of people get night-cramps, usually in the legs. Some have to jump out of bed and put their foot in warm water until the pain goes. Massage can also help. Cramp in the leg is very painful, but cramps can also be experienced in the heart muscle, stomach and intestines – and this is very frightening.

The only long-term solution is a diet rich in vitamins and minerals, with no dairy products and animal fat, and with plenty of green salads – and including two teaspoons of cider vinegar in a large glass of water twice daily. This treatment dissolves the acid crystals in the blood and passes them out through the kidneys; it also supplies to the body the all-important minerals such as potassium and calcium.

Cider vinegar for corns and calluses

Corns and calluses usually affect the feet, and can be very uncomfortable. First soak the feet in warm water, to which has been added half a cupful of Epsom salts (otherwise known as magnesium sulphate salts). Dry the feet. Soak a piece of lint in neat cider vinegar and cover the affected parts. Leave for approximately 30 minutes. Wash the cider vinegar off and dry the feet well; then rub briskly with a rough, dry towel.

Cider vinegar for dry scalps and dandruff

Those little white flakes which appear on the scalp and hair can be so embarrassing and irritating. Nobody knows the real cause but my opinion, as a nutritionist, is that the condition is systemic and first and foremost, the sufferer should adopt a diet of fresh fruit and vegetables, wholemeal bread and a high-protein content of nuts, beans, chicken, and lean meat. A high-protein diet should always be accompanied by an acid drink – cider vinegar. It is the best of all acid drinks because of the large amount of minerals it supplies to the body. Sugar and starch products, fatty and highly spiced foods, should be avoided. When the hair is washed, a final rinse of lukewarm water, to which half a cup of cider vinegar has been added, is very beneficial. A good multi-vitamin supplement is also desirable.

Cider vinegar for sleeplessness

It is very important to get a good night's sleep. If you get a good night's sleep, you can tackle any hard work the next day. For most people, a good night's sleep works wonders. Almost everyone experiences sleeplessness from time to time, for one reason or another. There are no rules about how much sleep is necessary but, for an adult, eight hours each night is accepted as normal. Lack of sleep causes irritability, nervousness, lack of concentration. Everything becomes an effort, and overtiredness leads to exhaustion and depression. Stress and tension can be the cause, and prolonged stress leads to a very depleted nervous system.

It is very important to remember that drugs do not cure sleeplessness – in fact, some sleep-inducing tablets have an effect whereby the more one takes of them, the less effective they are. There is also fear of addiction, which is most undesirable.

For the treatment of insomnia (sleeplessness):

1 Fresh air and exercise are very important, as is a good diet and perhaps a good multi-vitamin supplement.
2 Listening to music can be very beneficial and relaxing before bed-time.
3 Take a warm bath containing rosemary oil, or some other relaxing oil.
4 Make sure your bed is comfortable.
5 Keep regular sleeping hours.
6 Never take tea, coffee or any alcoholic drink before going to bed.
7 Make sure your room is well-ventilated, quiet and peaceful.
8 Have a light snack before going to bed, but never have a big meal.

9 Have some honey, which is a wonderful relaxant, soothing and feeding the nerves.

Before going to bed, heat half a tumbler of water and dissolve two teaspoons of clear honey in it. To this, add two teaspoons of cider vinegar and put the drink by your bed. Take a few sips as you get into bed. Then lie down in peace, thanking God for all that he has given you and asking for his blessing. It never fails to bring peace to me. If you wake in the night, take a sip of your honey-and-cider-vinegar concoction, and finish off the rest when you wake up.

Cider vinegar for varicose veins

Many of our patients suffer from varicose veins. Being arthritic, many of them become overweight. Movement is so painful that they stand or sit much of the time. The circulation becomes poor and, as a result, the blood in the veins becomes very sluggish. The surface veins can also become affected and often they can be very painful.

Sometimes there are distended veins in the lower bowel. These are called piles. Sometimes they come outside the rectum and often, too, they bleed. It is important for the sufferer to have a good diet and vitamin C, vitamin E and lecithin to aid the blood flow.

Varicose veins can become inflamed, causing pain. This is called phlebitis. A large, painful lump can be felt in the leg-vein and, sometimes ulcers can develop. Sometimes, the patient is advised to wear a tight stocking. In my opinion, this is the wrong line of treatment as it can hinder circulation. One patient who came to the clinic had suffered with a varicose ulcer for years. A plaster of Paris had been put on the leg from knee to ankle. The patient was in extreme pain. I removed the plaster and found that a lot of fluid had collected in the ankle. I dressed the ulcer with cream containing vitamin E and royal jelly, and a crepe bandage – not too tight – and, with dietary advice, the ulcer had healed in two weeks.

I advise my patients to use the following cider-vinegar treatment for their varicose veins. Cup the hand, pour in neat cider vinegar and massage the legs upwards three times daily. It takes time, sometimes months, but some of the results are amazing. Cider vinegar taken internally (two teaspoonfuls in plenty of water, three times daily) thins the blood and prevents it from clotting. In my opinion, this is much better than the half-aspirin prescribed for blood which is too thick.

Cider vinegar for constipation

Constipation is the failure to pass solid waste-matter, known as stools or faeces. There are many causes of this, but basically they can be grouped into three types: dietary deficiencies; mechanical obstruction to the passage of food along the bowel; or faulty bowel-habits.

a Dietary deficiencies

The waste-matter is the indigestible part of food. If the diet is low in vegetable fibre (found in fruits, bran and vegetables) there may be insufficient bulk of waste in the bowel to form more than the occasional stool. Starvation also causes constipation.

b Mechanical obstruction

Mechanical obstruction can occur because of narrowing of the bowel-tube by inflammation or tumour. Such a condition usually requires an operation to remedy it.

c Faulty bowel-habits

Faulty bowel-habits (e.g. retention of faeces, lack of daily exercise) are usually the main cause of constipation. A good diet, containing plenty of fruit and vegetables (raw if possible), is necessary. Two teaspoons of caster oil, to which has been added one teaspoon of cider vinegar, every morning before breakfast, should produce normal bowel-movement in a very short time. All refined and processed food should be eliminated from the diet. All tea, coffee, sugared and fizzy drinks should be avoided.

Constipation is all about the elimination of waste-matter and toxins. The constipated person is liable to succumb to all sorts of diseases because of the re-absorption of toxins from the bowel into the bloodstream. A purified body is a healthy body, fit and able to do the work for which it is destined.

Using complementary treatments safely

There are many complementary therapies available today, and many people turn to one or other of these therapies when they find that orthodox medicine has failed them. There are many reasons why people forsake their GP and set out to help themselves. Many television programmes have been broadcast relating, for example, to arthritis and orthodox treatments for it; a number of books have also been published setting out the side-effects of drugs. The public are becoming very aware, and unfortunately some people are losing faith in the medical profession.

I run a very successful clinic for arthritic patients – but I like my patients to have been diagnosed as having arthritis before they contact me. This means that, first and foremost, they contact their GP. I do not presume to diagnose their condition. On their first appointment, the X-rays and blood tests, which have been carried out in the GP's surgery and at the hospital, are a valuable source of information to me.

So many of my patients suffer with so many different conditions – and are on drugs for these conditions – that it is imperative that they are properly diagnosed in the first instance. I practise nutritional therapy, which works very well when used correctly. There are times when I should like to give a particular vitamin or mineral supplement, but because of the patient's history or diagnosis I cannot safely do so. For example, if I have a patient with poor circulation, my thoughts turn to a dosage of 800 International Units of vitamin E – so good for poor circulation – until on further investigation, I learn that my patient has a heart condition, so I must not exceed 400 International Units. Another example is vitamin D, which promotes calcium absorption, but too much of which can become toxic.

The saying, 'You are what you eat', is very true – though in my opinion, 'You are what you absorb', would be more accurate. In the nutritional field, many vitamins and minerals are not absorbed unless they are taken in conjunction with another. For instance, iron cannot be absorbed if vitamin C is not taken with it; vitamin E works well if taken with selenium; calcium will not work without vitamin D.

Having practised nutritional therapy for years, I should like to emphasize that, in my therapy at least, a correct diagnosis from the GP is invaluable, and should always be sought primarily. In addition, we often seek to work with GPs. In my clinic, treatment consists of diet, exercise and supplementary nutrition. The treatment varies from patient to patient, according to individual needs and, if necessary, we liaise with the patient's doctor. As a rule, the doctor proves very helpful and usually carries out any tests required. Many people have heart-trouble, angina, high blood pressure, thyroid problems, and many more conditions where the GP's help is invaluable.

Sometimes patients come to my clinic having already tried several of the alternative therapies which are currently available. In my opinion, the reason that patients do not get results is that they often do not give the therapy enough time. I tell my patients not to expect an overnight miracle: it will not happen. The treatment has to be practised every day until all signs and symptoms have cleared, and then for three months afterwards.

It is vital that the treatment is carried out as directed, and that the practitioner is kept fully informed of any irregularities arising during treatment – (e.g. weight-change, diarrhoea, constipation – any symptoms unusual for the individual) so that adjustments may be made as time goes by.

I like my patients to keep in touch with the hospital and their consultant rheumatologist, for two reasons. First, as a rule, the consultant does occasional blood tests which are very informative for him and for me. Second, in the vast majority of cases, those blood tests prove to my patients that their health has taken a turn for the better. It is very encouraging for patients to compare the results with those of previous blood tests, and to find improvement. Then they really know that they are on the road to recovery.

When the patient has been cleared of all signs and symptoms of their arthritis, we prescribe a reduced nutrition programme for the rest of their lives. They may go back to a normal diet, continuing to take a reduced quantity of their cider-vinegar drinks. The programme is designed to keep down the acid-levels in the body – ensuring the patients are free of arthritis, in other words. It works very well.

In my opinion, most diseases are constitutional in character – that is, disease only attacks people whose bodily condition is poor as a result of poor diet and/or wrong living. Strict diet, fresh air, and all measures for building up the body, are required. Sun and plenty of fresh air are excellent, as are Epsom-salt baths, along with any necessary extra treatment which the therapist considers necessary to bring about good health.

I always advise my patients to inform their doctors that they are taking my cider-vinegar treatment for their arthritis. A lot of doctors seem not to know what a wonderful treatment it is for arthritis and for dissolving the uric acid in the body. They often confuse it with cider or with malt vinegar, both of which are extremely acidic and can be very injurious to the patient.

Daily dosage

I have used cider vinegar for the past 35 years for me and my family. I have never known it to fail with my family and, since treating arthritic patients in my clinic – who present me with various conditions apart from arthritis – I have found very few adverse reactions to it. In my opinion, natural organic cider vinegar is one of nature's perfect drinks.

The amount to take varies from person to person – but the normal prescribed dosage is one dessertspoonful in a large glass of water, three times daily. However, for a person with *one kidney*, it is imperative that the dosage is drastically reduced because of the fact that cider vinegar is a natural diuretic. Having said that, it is a wonderful medicine for dissolving kidney stones. In such a case, I ask my patient to take one teaspoonful twice daily in a large glass of water. Patients with any kidney problems should have the reduced dosage.

There are certain other conditions which necessitate a reduced daily dosage of cider vinegar, as follows.

Patients on water-tablets

A very reduced prescription is in order because of the diuretic quality of the cider vinegar. If I were to give patients on water-tablets the normal cider-vinegar dosage, they would be incessantly passing urine, and that would cause them a great deal of stress. I give these patients potassium tablets to replace the potassium which the water-tablets are flushing out of the system.

Heart disease

Patients who have had heart problems sometimes need to take oral anticoagulants such as warfarin. These are prescribed in order to keep the blood flowing easily through the blood-vessels, by thinning the blood. As cider vinegar can also normalize blood which is too thick, this can exacerbate the effect of warfarin. People taking such drugs need to be monitored when taking cider vinegar. Patients who take cider vinegar can sometimes reduce their dosage of warfarin, under the doctor's guidance, which can only be helpful considering the harmful side-effects that warfarin can produce.

Possible adverse reactions to cider vinegar

If too much cider vinegar is taken, patients can lose weight. They do not realize that the cider vinegar is responsible, and begin to worry. Their families and friends worry because of the weight-loss, until eventually they go to the doctor, who is baffled, can find nothing wrong – and everybody is confused.

Such patients have heard that cider vinegar is good for arthritis and, without seeking informed help, they consume too much. If they had told the doctor that they were taking cider vinegar, the doctor may have realized that the diuretic properties of cider vinegar have caused the weight-loss. It is not until the patient rings the Margaret Hills Clinic and asks for advice that we recognize what has gone on. We regulate the intake, and the patient starts to put on weight again. We get a few such patients at the clinic.

The information we send out to our patients from the clinic categorically advises them to 'inform your doctor that you are having this treatment'. Some patients do not tell their doctors because they are frightened of the doctor's reaction. That, we can do nothing about.

I often think that, if the doctors could see the hundreds of letters that come in from our patients thanking us for their better health, they would have no hesitation in encouraging patients to do our treatment, or at least to contact the clinic for advice.

Candidiasis

This is a fungal disorder most commonly called thrush. It is caused by an excess amount of the yeast-like fungus, *Candida albicans*, which lives on the skin and the vulva, and in the mouth, bowel and vagina. Normally the fungus is harmless. However, it sometimes sets up an infection characterized by sore white patches which usually affect the mouth or vagina.

Thrush is particularly prevalent in babies, elderly people, diabetics, pregnant women and those taking antibiotics. It is also common where the immune system is not functioning properly, for example in people with AIDS or leukaemia, or those taking steroid drugs.

Thrush infection of the vulva is common, recurrent and troublesome. It causes itching and soreness with a white vaginal discharge. See your doctor, get it diagnosed and, if it is true thrush, your doctor will prescribe your treatment. Do not take vinegar or cider vinegar in your diet, and steer clear of antibiotics, if possible, when suffering from thrush.

We find quite often among our patients that antibiotics cause thrush. In my opinion, antibiotics should not be prescribed as liberally as they often seem to be. Once a patient has thrush, it is very difficult to get rid of and prevention is better than cure. My advice would be that people at risk of thrush take Acidophilus (available in health food shops) to support the immune system and prevent, if possible, the occurrence of thrush.

Other conditions

Other instances when the dosage of cider vinegar is drastically reduced to begin with are a hiatus hernia and/or a stomach ulcer. Cider vinegar to an ulcer can be compared to rubbing salt into a wound – it stings. However, at the end of the day, it is a fantastic healer – just like the salt.

One teaspoon of cider vinegar, well-diluted in a half-pint of water, daily, is prescribed until the patient can gradually take the required amount. This would be necessary in any individual case to bring about good health.

3

Cider vinegar in the home

The daily intake of cider vinegar helps to correct and maintain the body's acid-alkaline balance. Apples are very helpful for the human body – whether in the form of apple juice or cider vinegar, treatment results are excellent. No other vinegars can produce the same results as cider vinegar, and for so many conditions.

The vinegar should be made from crushed whole apples. It is very important to read the labels on the cider-vinegar bottle to ensure that it is made from crushed whole apples and not from apple peelings and cores as some vinegars are.

When I make soups, stews and casseroles, I feel that a vital, health-giving ingredient is omitted if I forget to add at least two teaspoons of cider vinegar. When vinegar is required in a recipe, I always use cider vinegar. In this way, I know that all my family are getting a wonderfully healthy diet. I have never had a case of food poisoning in the family, and I believe that, while I keep adding cider vinegar to the food, I never will.

Cider vinegar is excellent with vegetables and other food, such as lamb, for making mint sauce, etc. It is also a most cooling, refreshing summer drink. Add one dessertspoonful of cider vinegar to a large glass of cold water, and sip.

We build and rebuild our bodies through the food we eat, the fluids we drink and the air we breathe. Sickness is a signpost telling us that we have wandered off the road to health, and we must do something to put it right.

I have been trained in orthodox medicine, and I have studied and practised the alternative, natural method of healing for the past 50 years – first in my own family and then in treating many and varied conditions in my clinic. In my experience, the natural way is the best way. Drugs (as prescribed in orthodox medicine) suppress symptoms, and, in so doing, can often cause irreversible damage to the body. Natural treatments heal gently.

Always remember that two teaspoons of cider vinegar in a glass of water with or before each meal will ensure an excellent potassium-enriched meal. But in this chapter, I also want to tell you various ways of making cider vinegar palatable, using it in different recipes. We will also look at its uses throughout the house in different situations.

In winter, especially, soup is very satisfying. Summer soups can be delicious too – but on a cold winter's evening, after a day's work, there is nothing quite so warming as a bowl of nourishing soup. The following are some quick and easy recipes that can be made in advance and frozen if you wish.

SOUPS

Cream of potato soup

Serves 4

1 450 g / 1 lb potatoes
2 celery stalks
450 ml / ¾ pint water
pepper to taste
300 ml / ½ pint milk
2 tablespoons finely chopped
  parsley

1 large onion
40 g / 1½ oz butter
1 teaspoon salt
25 g / 1 oz cornflour
2 teaspoons cider vinegar

Slice the potatoes thinly, then slice the onion and celery. Fry the vegetables very gently in butter in a saucepan for 10 minutes. Do not allow to brown. Add water, salt and pepper. Bring to the boil. Cover the pan and simmer very gently for 45 minutes. Liquidize, or rub through a sieve, and return to the pan. Mix the cornflour to a smooth paste with a little of the cold milk and stir in the remainder. Add to the soup and bring to the boil, stirring. Simmer for 5 minutes. Remove from the heat and add the cider vinegar. Sprinkle with parsley and serve.

Cider Vinegar in borscht

Serves 6

1 medium-sized onion
450 g / 1 lb raw beetroot,
  sliced
1.1 litres / 2 pints vegetable
  stock
1 teaspoon yeast extract (e.g.
  Marmite)

1 small potato, halved
25 g / 1 oz butter / margarine
3 tablespoons cider vinegar
a little soured cream and
  chopped parsley to garnish

Chop the vegetables, melt the butter, and sauté the onion until transparent. Then add the potato, beetroot and stock, and bring to the boil. Reduce the heat, cover and simmer for 30 minutes. Allow to cool before blending, in small amounts, in a liquidizer. Return to the saucepan; add the remaining ingredients and season. Reheat to serving temperature; stir in the soured cream and chopped parsley before serving.

Carrot soup

Serves 4–6

450 g / 1 lb carrots
1 medium-sized onion
1 teaspoon dried thyme
1.1 litres / 2 pints vegetable
  stock
1 teaspoon yeast extract

1 medium-sized potato
25 g / 1 oz butter / margarine
1 teaspoon dried sage
2 teaspoons cider vinegar
salt and pepper

Chop the vegetables. Melt the butter in a saucepan, add the onion and sauté. Add the remaining ingredients, and bring to the boil. Reduce the heat and simmer, covered, for 30 minutes; then add the cider vinegar and blend in small quantities in a liquidizer, until the soup is smooth.

Red pottage

Serves 6

225 g / ½ lb haricot beans
1 beetroot, peeled and thinly
  sliced
2 onions, chopped
2.2 litres / 4 pints water

100 g / ¼ lb tomatoes, chopped
25 g / 1 oz butter
2 sticks celery, chopped
2 teaspoons cider vinegar

Soak the beans in cold water for 24 hours; then put the beans into 4 pints of cold water and bring to the boil. Add the butter. When the soup comes to the boil, add the tomatoes, celery and onions and beetroot. Allow to simmer for 2½ hours, then liquidize or put all through a wire sieve and add cider vinegar. Reheat and serve.

Fennel soup

Serves 4

25 g / 1 oz butter / margarine
1 large fennel bulb
300 ml / ½ pint vegetable stock
1 teaspoon cider vinegar
chopped parsley to garnish

1 medium-sized onion
1 medium-sized potato
450 mg / ¾ pint milk
seasoning to taste

Melt the butter in a saucepan and sauté the onion until transparent. Add the chopped fennel and chopped potato. Stir well. Add the stock and bring to the boil. Cover and simmer for about 30 minutes; allow to cool and purée in a liquidizer. Return to the saucepan and add milk, cider vinegar, and salt and pepper to taste. If too thick, add more stock; reheat, but do not boil. To garnish, sprinkle with chopped parsley.

French onion soup

Serves 4

350 g / 12 oz onions, chopped   12 g / ½ oz butter / margarine
a pinch of sugar   1 beef-stock cube
1.1 litres / 2 pints water   2 teaspoons cider vinegar
1 small French loaf   50 g / 2 oz Parmesan cheese

Fry the onions in butter until they are very brown. Sprinkle on a little sugar to caramelize them. Dissolve the stock-cube in 2 pints of boiling water, and pour this over the onions, stirring well. Bring to the boil, withdraw from heat, add the cider vinegar and stir well. Serve with toasted French bread sprinkled with Parmesan cheese.

Pea soup

Serves 4

450 g / 1 lb fresh peas, shelled   1 chicken stock-cube
40 g / 1½ oz butter   1 teaspoon cider vinegar
sprig of mint

Cook the peas in a very minimum amount of water, and liquidize. Dissolve the chicken stock-cube in 2 pints of boiling water. Put into the saucepan with the pea purée and bring to boiling point. Stir in cider vinegar, butter and the sprig of mint.

Red bean soup

Serves 4

225 g / 8 oz red kidney beans
1 clove garlic, crushed
25 g / 1 oz parsley, finely
  chopped
2 teaspoons cider vinegar

1.1 litres / 2 pints water
1 tablespoon olive oil
salt and pepper to taste

Soak the kidney beans overnight, then drain them and put them into a heavy saucepan with 2 pints of cold water. Boil for 10 minutes, then simmer for 1 hour. Remove half the beans from the pan with a slotted spoon and purée in a food processor. Season to taste. Return the purée to the saucepan to keep warm. Sauté the chopped garlic in the olive oil in a small frying pan until golden. Stir in some chopped parsley, drain and add to the soup. Bring back to the boil; remove from heat and stir in the cider vinegar; then serve.

Cider vinegar and lentil soup

Serves 4

175 g / 6 oz red lentils
1.1 litres / 2 pints water
100 g / 4 oz onions, chopped
1 clove garlic, chopped
salt and pepper to taste

1 chicken stock-cube
1 tablespoon cider vinegar
1 medium-sized carrot,
  chopped

Soak the lentils overnight in stock made from 2 pints of water and the chicken stock-cube. Put the garlic, onion and carrot into a saucepan, and add a quarter of a cup of stock in which the lentils have been soaking. Cover and cook over a low heat until soft. Add the lentils and remaining liquid. Season, and bring to the boil; cover and simmer for 1 hour. Add the cider vinegar and serve.

Parsnip and apple soup

Serves 6

225 g / 8 oz parsnips
50 g / 2 oz butter
1.1 litres / 2 pints water
salt and pepper
150 ml / ¼ pint single cream

1 cooking apple
1 chicken stock-cube
1 bay leaf
2 teaspoons cider vinegar
chopped parsley

Peel and chop the parsnips finely. Peel, core and cube the apple. Sweat parsnips and apple in a saucepan with the butter; cover and cook over a low heat for 10 minutes, stirring from time to time. Make up 1.1 litres (2 pints) of stock by dissolving the chicken stock-cube in boiling water, and add to the pan. Add the bay leaf; season and simmer until the parsnip is tender. Take out the bay leaf; put the liquid in a food processor and blend to a smooth texture. Reheat and add 2 teaspoons of cider vinegar; add the cream and stir gently. Sprinkle on chopped parsley, then serve at once.

Liver and bacon soup

Serves 4

1 medium-sized onion
25 g / 1 oz butter
25 g / 1 oz flour
$\frac{1}{2}$ teaspoon salt
$\frac{1}{2}$ teaspoon Worcester sauce

225 g / 8 oz lean bacon
225 g / 8 oz liver
900 ml / 1$\frac{1}{2}$ pints water
1 dessertspoon cider vinegar
1 tablespoon chopped parsley
to garnish

Finely chop the onion and bacon. Fry gently in butter in the frying pan for 5–7 minutes. Wash the liver well and wipe dry; cut it into half-inch cubes, toss in flour until each piece is well coated, add to the pan and fry with onion and bacon for a further 5 minutes, stirring all the time. Gradually blend in the water; add salt and Worcester sauce; bring slowly to the boil while stirring. Lower the heat and cover the pan. Simmer gently for 1$\frac{1}{2}$ hours. Remove from the heat; add the cider vinegar, then ladle into four warm soup-bowls. Garnish with chopped parsley.

Cabbage soup

Serves 4

225 g / 8 oz cabbage
25 g / 1 oz butter
salt and pepper to taste
1 dessertspoon cider vinegar

1 medium-sized onion
600 ml / 1 pint beef stock
3 tablespoons soured cream
finely chopped parsley

Shred the cabbage finely, wash and drain well. Coarsely grate the onion. Melt butter in a saucepan, and fry the onion gently until soft and pale gold. Add the cabbage and stock, and bring to the boil. Season to taste with salt and pepper, reduce the heat and cover the pan. Simmer gently for 15 minutes, then remove from the heat and add the cider vinegar and soured cream. Sprinkle with parsley and serve hot.

SALAD DRESSINGS

Salad dressings are an ideal way of introducing cider vinegar into the daily diet. They really do make salads delicious and nourishing. Different dressings add variety and a range of different tastes to an otherwise mundane salad. The following is a basic cider vinegar dressing. All quantities of dressings serve 4–6 people.

Salad dressing

For green and mixed salads, potato salads, meat, poultry, fish, cheese and egg salads

1 carton 142 ml (5 fl oz) soured cream
1 tablespoon cider vinegar
$\frac{1}{4}$ teaspoon salt
1 tablespoon milk
1 teaspoon caster sugar
a shake of pepper

Beat the soured cream, milk and cider vinegar together, stir in the sugar, and season to taste with salt and pepper. If a thinner dressing is preferred, add a little extra milk. Leave for 15 minutes in a cool place before using.

Soured cream with chives dressing

Follow the recipe and method for the basic soured cream dressing, and stir in one heaped tablespoon of snipped chives before seasoning with salt and pepper.

Soured cream and parsley dressing

Follow the recipe and method for the basic soured cream dressing, and stir in one heaped tablespoon of finely chopped parsley before seasoning with salt and pepper.

Soured cream with mustard dressing

For beef, ham and tongue salads and salads and with canned fish

Follow the recipe and method for the basic soured cream dressing, and add 1 level teaspoon of made mustard with the cider vinegar.

Soured cream with horseradish dressing

For cold roast beef and salad

Follow the recipe and method for the basic soured cream dressing, and stir in 2 level teaspoons of grated horseradish before seasoning with salt and pepper.

Soured cream with cucumber dressing

For all poultry and fish salads

Follow the recipe and method for the basic soured cream dressing, and stir in 4 level tablespoons of very finely grated, peeled cucumber; then season with salt and pepper.

Soured cream with tomato dressing

For vegetable, poultry, fish, and egg salads

Follow the recipe and method for basic soured cream dressing, and stir in 1 dessertspoon of tomato purée and 1 finely chopped, skinned tomato; then season with salt and pepper.

Soured cream with lemon dressing

For poultry, fish and egg salads

Follow the recipe and method for soured cream dressing, and stir in 1 level teaspoon of finely grated lemon-peel; then season with salt and pepper.

Paprika dressing

For veal, poultry and egg salads

Follow the recipe and method for soured cream dressing, and stir in 2 level teaspoons of paprika; then season with salt and pepper.

Nut dressing

Follow the recipe and method for basic soured cream dressing, and add 50 g / 2 oz of finely chopped walnuts or finely chopped salted almonds; then season with salt and pepper.

Dairy salad dressing

For green and mixed salads, salads with white fish, poultry, eggs or cheese

4 tablespoons milk
4 tablespoons olive oil
$\frac{1}{4}$ level teaspoon mustard
pepper

4 tablespoons cider vinegar
$\frac{1}{2}$ level teaspoon caster sugar
$\frac{1}{4}$ level teaspoon salt

Beat the milk, cider vinegar and oil together until smooth and well-blended; then beat in the sugar, mustard and salt, and season to taste with pepper.

Cream cheese dressing

For green and mixed salads, salads with poultry, fish or eggs

100 g/4 oz cream cheese
$\frac{1}{4}$ level teaspoon salt
3 teaspoons cider vinegar

1 tablespoon fresh single cream
$\frac{1}{2}$ level teaspoon caster sugar

Put the cream cheese into a bowl, and gradually blend in the cream; stir in the remaining ingredients and put into the fridge for 15 minutes before using. If thinner dressing is preferred, add a little more cream.

You can vary this recipe by adding half a teaspoon of celery-salt instead of salt, or half a teaspoon of garlic-salt instead of salt, or 1 level teaspoon of finely grated onion.

Mayonnaise is delicious made with cider vinegar. The following is a basic mayonnaise which can be varied according to taste – there are many possibilities.

Basic mayonnaise

2 standard eggs, yolks only
½ level teaspoon salt
¼ teaspoon Worcester sauce
300 ml / ½ pint olive oil
1 tablespoon boiling water

½ level teaspoon dry mustard
½ level teaspoon caster sugar
a shake of pepper
2 tablespoons cider vinegar

Put the egg-yolks, mustard, salt, sugar, Worcester sauce and pepper into a bowl and beat until smooth. Beating more quickly, add 150 ml / ¼ pint of oil – a drop at a time – and continue beating until the mayonnaise is very thick; then stir in one tablespoon of cider vinegar. Beat in the rest of the oil gradually, about a dessertspoonful at a time. When all the oil has been added, stir in the last tablespoon of cider vinegar and the boiling water (the water helps to prevent separation). Adjust seasoning to taste, then transfer to a covered container. This mayonnaise will keep in the fridge for two weeks.

The following are possible variations on the above.

Aïoli mayonnaise

For all vegetable salads, salads with hard-boiled eggs, beef and lamb

To the basic mayonnaise mixture, add one very finely chopped clove of garlic after stirring in the boiling water.

Camilla mayonnaise

For cold poultry, fish and egg salad

Stir 142 ml / 5 fl oz of soured cream into the mayonnaise before stirring in the boiling water.

Green dragon mayonnaise

For all cold fish and shellfish dishes

Mince finely 1 garlic clove, 3 anchovy fillets, 2 tablespoons of chives and a handful of parsley; then add these to the basic mayonnaise after stirring in boiling water. Blend in 1 dessertspoon each of cider vinegar and lemon juice, and 142 ml / 5 fl oz of soured cream; then adjust salt and pepper to taste.

Chantilly mayonnaise

For cold poultry and egg salads

Stir 150 ml / $\frac{1}{4}$ pint of fresh, whipped double cream into the basic mayonnaise mixture before stirring in the boiling water.

Curry mayonnaise

For cold poultry and egg salads

After stirring in the boiling water, add to the basic mayonnaise mixture 2 level teaspoons of curry powder, 1 level teaspoon of finely grated onion, a pinch of cayenne pepper and a level tablespoon of sweet pickle.

Louis mayonnaise

For cold shellfish and winter vegetable salads

After stirring in the boiling water, add to the basic mayonnaise mixture 3 tablespoons of fresh double cream, 2–3 tablespoons of bottled chilli sauce, 1 teaspoon of Worcester sauce, half a small green pepper (finely chopped), 1 level tablespoon of finely grated onion and 3 dessertspoons of lemon juice.

Russian mayonnaise

For green and mixed salads, cold shellfish and egg dishes

After stirring in boiling water, add to the basic mayonnaise mixture 142 ml / 5 fl oz soured cream, 1 dessertspoon of bottled chilli sauce, 2 level tablespoons of finely chopped canned pimento, 1 teaspoon of cider vinegar, 1 level teaspoon of paprika and 1 large hard-boiled egg, chopped.

Spanish mayonnaise

For green and egg salads

After stirring in the boiling water, add to the basic mayonnaise mixture 2 level tablespoons of tomato purée and 3 level tablespoons of finely chopped canned pimento.

Swedish mayonnaise

For cold pork, lamb and mutton dishes and cold sausage platters

After stirring in boiling water, add to the basic mayonnaise mixture 150 ml / $\frac{1}{4}$ pint of thick, unsweetened apple purée, 1 or 2 level teaspoons of grated horseradish and 5 tablespoons of soured cream.

Tartar mayonnaise

For fried dishes

After stirring in boiling water, add to the basic mayonnaise mixture 1 level tablespoon each of finely chopped capers and parsley; then add 2 tablespoons of finely chopped gherkins.

Mayonnaise verte

For cold salmon and salmon trout

Mince very finely a handful of parsley and 2 level tablespoons each of fresh tarragon and chives, two heaped tablespoons of torn-up spinach and 2 level tablespoons of watercress. Add to the basic mayonnaise mixture after stirring in boiling water.

Tivoli mayonnaise

For poultry, tongue, ham, fish and egg salads

Add 1 carton (142 ml / 5 fl oz) of natural yoghurt to the basic mayonnaise mixture, before stirring in the boiling water.

French dressing

For all tossed salads

4 tablespoons olive oil or corn
  oil
$\frac{1}{2}$ level teaspoon caster sugar
$\frac{1}{4}$ teaspoon Worcester sauce

$\frac{1}{2}$ level teaspoon salt
$\frac{1}{2}$ level teaspoon dry mustard
2 tablespoons cider vinegar

Put the oil, salt, sugar, mustard and Worcester sauce into a basin, beat until smooth, then gradually beat in the vinegar. Continue beating until the dressing thickens.

Blue Stilton dressing

For all green and mixed salads

Gradually beat French dressing into 2 oz finely mashed blue Stilton.

Ravigotte

For cold meat salads

Add to the French dressing 1 level tablespoon of finely grated onion, 1 level dessertspoon of finely chopped capers, 1 heaped tablespoon of finely chopped parsley, and $\frac{1}{2}$ a level teaspoon each of finely chopped fresh chervil and tarragon. Mix well.

PICKLES AND CHUTNEYS

Pickles and chutneys are always very popular, but very often we buy them at considerable expense not realizing how easy they are to make. Pickles and chutneys are the classic accompaniment to cold meats and cheeses. The main preserving agent for pickles is vinegar. The type of vinegar used is very important. Malt vinegar is cheap and has a good flavour; white vinegar is less strongly flavoured. Red or white wine vinegar is used sometimes – but in my opinion there is nothing to equal cider vinegar for its health-giving properties and unique flavour. Spices used in pickling are usually left whole so as not to cloud the vinegar. In chutneys, spices are usually ground. Pickles are generally cooked briefly or not at all, so that the fruit and vegetables retain their crispness. Chutneys are cooked for a considerable time, but not for too long. If they are allowed to become too thick they may dry out when bottled.

The following recipes are an ideal way of incorporating cider vinegar into your diet, allowing you to benefit from its health-giving qualities.

Sweet apple pickles

Makes 1.5–2 g / 3–4 lbs

2.25 kg / 5 lb eating apples
300 ml / $\frac{1}{2}$ pint cider vinegar
6 whole cloves

450 g / 1 lb honey
$\frac{1}{2}$ teaspoon ground cinnamon

Peel and core the apples, and cut them into large cubes. Choose apples which will not pulp when cooked. Place the honey, vinegar, cinnamon and cloves in a saucepan and heat to boiling point. Then add small amounts of the apples and cook them in the syrup until they are transparent. Remove them with a slotted spoon and place them in sterilized jars. Repeat this process with the remaining apples. Pour the remaining syrup over the apples and seal in the usual way.

Apple and banana chutney

Makes about 2 kg / 4 lbs

450 g / 1 lb green cooking
   apples
100 g / 4 oz seedless raisins
2 bananas
350 g / 12 oz brown sugar
25 g / 1 oz salt

225 g / 8 oz onions
100 g / 4 oz crystallized ginger
150 ml / ¼ pint water
1 teaspoon ground allspice
1 teaspoon cider vinegar

Core but do not peel the apples; chop them, and the onions, raisins and ginger. Slice the bananas and place them with the apples, onions, raisins, ginger and water in a pan. Gently heat the mixture, cover and simmer until tender. Remove the pan from the heat and stir in the sugar, spice, seasoning and cider vinegar until the sugar has dissolved. Simmer slowly in an uncovered pan until the chutney is thick. While still hot, pour into sterilized jars and cover at once.

Spiced cider vinegar

Makes 1 litre / 1¾ pints

1 litre / 1¾ pints cider vinegar
1 teaspoon cloves
1 teaspoon black peppercorns
2 bay leaves

5 cm / 2-inch piece cinnamon
2 teaspoons allspice
1 teaspoon mustard seed

Place all ingredients in a saucepan, stir, cover and bring the vinegar almost to the boil (do not allow it actually to boil). Immediately remove from the heat and set aside for 3 hours. Strain the vinegar and, if it is not going to be used immediately, pour it into clean, dry bottles and seal.

Tarragon vinegar

Makes 1 litre / 1¾ pints

900 ml / 1½ pints cider vinegar
3 small Spanish onions

1 large stalk tarragon
a few black peppercorns

Fill a large preserving pan with the vinegar. Add the tarragon, onions and peppercorns. Seal and leave the vinegar to steep for 4 weeks. Strain the vinegar into sterilized bottles and seal.

Shallot vinegar

Makes 1 litre / 1¾ pints

8 shallots, trimmed
a few fresh bay leaves

1 sprig thyme
1 litre / 1¾ pints cider vinegar

Place all the ingredients in a large earthenware crock or jug. Cover and leave the vinegar to steep for 4 weeks. Strain the vinegar into clean bottles and seal.

Chow Chow

Makes 1 kg / 2 lbs

225 g / 8 oz cucumber, cut
  into 2 cm / ¾ inch cubes
225 g / 8 oz French beans
1 small celery heart
225 g / 8 oz under-ripe
  tomatoes, sliced
900 ml / 1½ pints spiced cider
  vinegar

100 g / 2 oz green peppers,
  chopped
2 medium-sized onions
1 small cauliflower
salt

Place the cucumber, pepper and beans in a large bowl. Peel and thinly slice the onions, wash the celery sticks and cut into 1 cm / ½ inch pieces; break the cauliflower into small florets. Whisk all the vegetables together and sprinkle with salt. Cover and leave for 24 hours. Drain and rinse the vegetables in cold water. Dry them thoroughly before packing them into jars. Fill to the top with spiced vinegar. Cover in the usual way and leave to mature for 2 months before using.

Pickled onions

Makes 1 kg / 2 lbs

2 kg / 4 lbs silver-skinned
   onions
2.2 litres / 4 pints water

450 g / 1 lb salt
1 litre / 1¾ pints spiced cider
   vinegar

Wash the unpeeled onions and place them in a bowl. Mix half of the salt with half of the water, and pour this brine over the onions. They should be completely covered. Cover them with a plate to ensure that they are totally immersed and leave for 12 hours. Drain and peel the onions and place them in a clean bowl. Mix the remaining salt and water and pour it over the onions. Cover and leave again for 24 hours. Drain and wash the onions; pack them into sterilized jars, leaving plenty of space at the top. Strain the spiced cider vinegar over the onions until there is at least 1.5 cm / ½ inch of vinegar above them. Cover and leave for 3 months.

Pickled lemons

Makes 12

12 large lemons
salt

1.7 litres / 3 pints spiced cider
   vinegar

Wash the lemons and peel thinly (the peel may be used for other recipes). Place the lemons in a bowl or large jar covering each layer with plenty of salt. Leave for 2 weeks. Wash off the salt and dry the lemons on absorbent kitchen paper; then arrange the lemons in preserving jars. Bring the vinegar to the boil and pour it over the lemons. Seal and leave it for 2 months. Serve with veal or chicken.

Pickled mushrooms

Makes about 450 g / 1 lb

450 g / 1 lb small mushrooms
1 teaspoon salt
2 blades mace
cider vinegar

1 tablespoon grated onion
1 teaspoon ground ginger
12 peppercorns

Cut the stalks off the mushrooms, level with the edges of their caps.
Wash the mushrooms well and drain them. Place the mushrooms,
and other ingredients, in a pan with enough cider vinegar to cover.
Bring to the boil and simmer gently until the mushrooms are tender.
Lift out the mushrooms and arrange them in layers in a preserving
jar. Cover them with the cider vinegar, seal and leave for 1 month
before using. Serve with cold spiced meats.

Spicy pickled red cabbage

Makes about 1.5 kg / 3 lb

1.5 kg / 3 lbs red cabbage,
  washed and shredded
1.1 litres / 2 pints cider vinegar
2 bay leaves
2 tablespoons pickling spice
10 black peppercorns

75 g / 3 oz salt
2 tablespoons sugar
3 cloves
$\frac{1}{2}$ teaspoon grated nutmeg
2 tablespoons coriander seeds

Mix the cabbage and salt in a bowl, cover and chill in the
refrigerator for 24 hours, stirring occasionally. Rinse the cabbage,
squeeze dry and pack it into sterilized jars. Place all the remaining
ingredients in a pan and heat gently, stirring until the sugar is
completely dissolved. Boil for 5 minutes then remove from the heat
and cool. Strain the liquid and pour into the jars to cover the
cabbage; add a few peppercorns and coriander seeds to each jar if
wished. Seal the jars and leave for 2 weeks before using.

Pickled peppers

6 large red peppers
6 black peppercorns
sprigs each of thyme, bay
   leaves and parsley

1 litre / $1\frac{3}{4}$ pints cider vinegar
$\frac{1}{2}$ teaspoon salt
4 tablespoons olive oil

Halve and de-seed the peppers, cut into large chunks and place in four sterilized jars. Heat the vinegar, spices and herbs in a pan and bring to the boil. Boil for 5 minutes, and then strain. Divide the vinegar between the four jars, and leave to cool. Add 1 tablespoon of oil to each jar before sealing.

Pickled aubergines

3 aubergines

spiced cider vinegar

Cut the aubergines in half lengthways and boil them in salted water for 2 minutes. Drain the aubergines, place in sterilized jars and cover with cold spiced cider vinegar. Seal and store for 2 weeks before using.

Mustard pickle

Makes 2.75 kg/6 lbs

1 small cucumber, chopped
700 g/1½ lb tomatoes, roughly
    chopped
150 g/6 oz salt
1 teaspoon ground ginger
1 teaspoon pickling spice
a few coriander seeds
100 g/4 oz seedless raisins

3 onions, chopped
1 large cauliflower, washed
    and divided into florets
600 ml/1 pint cider vinegar
1 teaspoon black pepper
2 teaspoons dry mustard
225 g/8 oz soft brown sugar

Layer the vegetables and salt in a bowl, cover with cold water and cover bowl with foil. Leave in a cool place for 24 hours. Rinse and drain the vegetables thoroughly; place them with the other ingredients in a large pan. Heat gently, stirring until the sugar has dissolved. Bring to the boil, then simmer until the vegetables are tender, stirring occasionally. Pour into sterilized jars and store in a cool place.

Spicy apple chutney

Makes about 2 kg / 4 lbs

450 g / 1 lb cooking apples,
  cored and chopped
225 g / 8 oz raisins
3 bananas, sliced
1 teaspoon allspice
½ teaspoon cayenne pepper
350 g / 12 oz brown sugar

2 small onions, chopped
100 g / 4 oz crystallized ginger,
  chopped
100 ml / 4 fl oz water
½ teaspoon grated nutmeg
2 tablespoons salt
600 ml / 1 pint cider vinegar

Place the apple, onion, raisins, ginger, bananas and water in a pan, cover with a lid and cook gently until tender. Add the remaining ingredients, and stir until the sugar has completely dissolved. Simmer until the chutney has thickened, stirring occasionally. Pour the hot chutney into sterilized jars and seal in the usual way. Serve with cold meats and cheese.

Mixed fruit chutney

Makes 1 kg / 2 lbs

225 g / 8 oz cooking apples
175 g / 6 oz dried apricots
350 g / 12 oz soft brown sugar
1 teaspoon garam masala
a small piece fresh root ginger,
  finely chopped
1 teaspoon cumin seeds

225 g / 8 oz pears
2 tablespoons sultanas or raisins
300 ml / ½ pint cider vinegar
8 cloves garlic, finely sliced
2 teaspoons salt

Peel and core the apples and pears. Cut the apples, pears and apricots into small pieces and place in a preserving pan with the remaining ingredients. Bring the mixture to the boil and boil gently for 40 minutes until the chutney is thick. Allow the chutney to cool before bottling and covering in the usual way.

Tomato chutney

Makes about 2 kg / 4 lbs

1 teaspoon pickling spice
300 ml / ½ pint cider vinegar
1 kg / 2 lbs tomatoes, green
* or red, sliced*
¼ teaspoon pepper
½ teaspoon ground ginger
225 g / 8 oz sugar

2 large onions, finely chopped
225 g / 8 oz apples, peeled,
* cored and chopped*
½ teaspoon salt
1 rounded teaspoon dry
* mustard*
225 g / 8 oz sultanas

Put the pickling spice into a piece of muslin. Place this, with the onions, in a saucepan with 4 tablespoons of the vinegar and simmer gently until onions are nearly soft. Add the prepared apples, tomatoes, salt, pepper, mustard, ginger and sultanas. Simmer gently until the mixture is quite soft, stirring from time to time. Add the remaining vinegar and the sugar. When the sugar has thoroughly dissolved, boil steadily until the chutney is the consistency of jam. Remove the muslin bag, pour the hot chutney into warmed jars and cover at once with waxed paper, then with a metal lid.

Cider vinegar around the house

Gleaming windows

Add half a cup (150 ml / a quarter of a pint) cider vinegar to half a bucket of warm or cold water, wipe over the windows and shine with a dry cloth to give a brilliant, no-smear shine.

Scalds and burns

Pour cider vinegar on the burnt part – it has an instant cooling effect. Soak a piece of lint in the cider vinegar and apply to the burn; it usually prevents any blisters forming.

Bee and wasp stings

Apply neat cider vinegar after the sting has been removed.

Sore throats

Add half a cupful to a pint of water and gargle three to four times daily; also add 1 dessertspoon to a glass of water and sip – it kills the virus in the sore throat.

Dull or out-of-condition hair

Add half a cupful of cider vinegar to the final rinse – you will be amazed at how your hair shines. Also, a little cider vinegar massaged into the hair morning and evening will improve its condition very quickly. However, it does tend to straighten permed hair.

Varicose veins

These can be very unsightly, but massaging with cider vinegar, poured into the palm of the hand, can really help. One of my patients massaged the veins of her lower legs morning and evening – in seven months they had reduced and practically disappeared. She also took cider-vinegar drinks three times daily – she was thrilled that her circulation was so much better as a result.

4

Crude black molasses and ho

As I go about my daily appointments I am horrified to note the awful side-effects of the various drugs prescribed for patients whose bodies are so depleted with ill-health that they can scarcely think. Stresses and strains of modern living take a dreadful toll on health. Patients are depressed and fearful. People of all ages come to our clinic – children, youngsters, middle-aged and elderly people, male and female – all with depleted bodies full of toxic acid.

I have found that the vast majority are constipated. A lot of people do not realize that constipation can seriously affect health because it prevents the elimination of toxins from the body. When these toxins are absorbed into the general circulation, the liver is not able to cope with them: a condition called toxaemia then occurs. In my opinion, the cause has to be treated before the symptoms, and, unless my patient is diabetic or very overweight, I suggest a teaspoon of crude black molasses three times daily. This, as a rule, brings about normal body functions and a daily elimination of toxins.

Constipation is a disease of modern times. When people get constipated, they resort to taking laxatives, which relieves the constipation for a little while, but in the long run makes the bowel lazy until it refuses to function without the laxative. (Note: if diarrhoea alternates with constipation, you should seek medical advice, for it could be a warning sign that some undesirable condition may be starting up in the intestines or lower bowel.)

Black molasses is full of iron and other minerals, and is a wonderful natural laxative. It is a wonderful feeling to have a regular bowel-movement which eliminates the stress and strain of sluggishness and piles.

Cane molasses is a deep-rooting grass. Its roots grow deep into the subsoil, absorbing essential ingredients from the rocks. It is also grown in soil not heavily impregnated with artificial fertilizers. Cane molasses contains appreciable quantities of vitamins B1 and B2 and is superior in every way to white sugar. Crude black molasses is the best known source of the B vitamins, ʉcularly B6. White sugars, by contrast, drain the body of vitamin B1 in particular, and have a damaging effect on the calcium-phosphorus content. Over the years, this damage can lead to a number of diseases such as arthritis, rheumatism, diabetes, etc. Many claims have been made recently for the benefits of taking black molasses. I find it very valuable in the healing of arthritis, polymyalgia and rheumatism in particular.

Figure 2 Analysis of black molasses, per 100 g.

water	22 g	sugars	10 mg
protein	1.89 g	phosphorus	55 g
calcium	580 mg	sodium	85 mg
iron	7.97 mg	thiamine	92 mg
potassium	1.85 g	niacin	275 mg
riboflavin	245 mg	pantothenic acid	4 mg
biotin	16 mg	magnesium	28 mg
pyridoxine	270 mg	calories	220 kcal

You can see from the analysis in Figure 2 that molasses is a wonderful product – but do beware of any molasses to which sulphur dioxide is added as a preservative.

Cider vinegar, honey and crude black molasses form the basis of treatment for arthritis at our clinic. Some patients mix the three together with hot (not boiling) water as a drink. Others eat a spoonful of molasses neat; others again mix the molasses with warm water, and having taken that, they mix the honey with hot water and add the specified amount of cider vinegar. For the overweight person we prescribe two tablespoons of cider vinegar, well diluted, three times daily. As a rule, the weight comes off very quickly. Those who are not overweight take one to two teaspoons of honey dissolved in a glass of hot water, to which is added one dessertspoon of cider vinegar. This is taken three times daily, in conjunction with as much honey as they wish. As a rule the cider vinegar normalizes body weight, and the honey is an excellent energy-producer, full of the B vitamins.

Molasses

Cane molasses and jaggery (coarse brown sugar made from date-palm sap) contain large quantities of vitamins B1 and B2, and are superior in every way to white sugar. It is also good to note from the analysis that black molasses contains large amounts of potassium (1.85 g per 100 g), as well as calcium, pantothenic acid, pyridoxine, riboflavin and thiamine. Apart from being a good laxative, it is a wonderful food for the nerves.

To eat molasses at every meal is not a good idea – it is easily digested, but some people's digestions are very weak and sensitive. Some people cannot take molasses at all – it gives them diarrhoea, especially if they are never constipated. I always advise my patients to regulate the dosage to suit them individually. A good breakfast to start the day could be two dessertspoons of wheat germ, one of bran, and a teaspoon of molasses, with hot or cold milk. The molasses can also be taken in hot water, or hot milk, or taken straight from the jar. It can be taken on bread, in cakes, puddings, tarts and desserts, and made into toffee.

Crude black cane molasses should replace sugar wherever possible. Sugar contains empty calories which are fattening and add weight – and being overweight is not good for the heart. The risk of heart attacks should be reduced by keeping slim, avoiding sugar and all foods made with sugar, and by avoiding animal fats. Replace them with unsaturated fats, such as margarine, sunflower, soya and olive oil fats. Exercise is also very important: gentle walking each day is good. If you have had a heart attack, go easy on the exercise. Swimming is good. Just do what you feel comfortable with. You should also give up smoking. The nicotine in cigarettes blocks the airways to the lungs, which throws extra strain on the heart. Last, but not least, avoid constipation and anything that would contribute to high blood pressure.

Excessive use of salt in the diet is not good. It can create high blood pressure. Eating small meals regularly is very desirable, and it is said that taking cider vinegar (two to three teaspoons in a glass of water, two to three times daily) can strengthen the heart muscles.

Molasses contains a good amount of calcium – 580 mg per 100 grams. A good number of our patients are going through the menopause or 'change of life'. A common problem is osteoporosis, or weakness of the bones, due to reduced oestrogen production which leads to calciumloss. Women with thyroid disorders are particularly prone to menopausal complaints, especially calcium loss. Here again, the taking of cider vinegar and molasses will help enormously with the calcium deficiency.

Hormone Replacement Therapy (HRT)

HRT is often prescribed by the medical profession – but in my opinion it may merely postpone symptoms and mask real problems, and it has been linked to a slightly increased risk of breast cancer, cancer of the uterus, stroke and also heart disease. It reduces zinc levels in the body, and increases the body's need of B-complex vitamins, vitamin E and other vitamins and minerals. Oestrogen is said to help in the treatment of osteoporosis – but this has not been proved and, in my opinion, it does more harm than good.

The relation of calcium deficiency to cramps is well-known. When molasses is taken, many patients report that the cramps disappear.

I also find that patients on HRT do not necessarily get the relief from arthritis that we normally expect from our combined treatment of cider vinegar, honey, molasses, a regulated diet and nutritional supplements. In my opinion, it is because HRT suppresses hot flushes and various other normal symptoms. It also prevents the elimination of acids from the body. Our mothers used to say, 'Every hot flush is worth a guinea' (£1.05). How right they were! Hot flushes relieve the body of so much acid, through the elimination of toxic acids in the skin, that I can see the reasoning behind that saying. At the end of the day, there is nothing to equal guided natural treatment for the vast majority of conditions. I say 'guided', because unless the patient has professional guidance, mistakes can be made, over-dosage even of natural products can happen, possibly making the patient worse.

Honey

For patients who are not diabetic or overweight, honey makes cider vinegar very palatable. I ask my patients to dissolve one or two teaspoons of honey in a 300 ml (half-pint) glass of hot (not boiling) water, add to this one or two dessertspoons of cider vinegar, and sip at any time of day. When allowed to go cold, this is a most refreshing summer cooler. Very often in the hot weather, I add two dessertspoons of cider vinegar to a glass of cold water – it is invaluable in dryness of the mouth and throat.

Honey is basically a solution of sugars which make up 79% of its weight.

Figure 3 Analysis of honey.

water	18%	dextrose	35%
fructose	40%	other sugars	4%
other substances	3%		

Constituent parts of the 3 per cent 'other substances' in honey are approximately 15 organic acids (including acetic, butyric, gluconic, malic and succinic acids); approximately 12 mineral elements (including potassium, calcium, sulphur, chlorine and iron); approximately 17 free amino acids (including proline, glutonic acid and lysine); and approximately 4–7 proteins.

Honey also contains an anti-bacterial substance, which has caused it to be used for wound-dressing. It does not dry out when applied to a wound and there is a complete lack of any side-effects on healthy tissue.

There are several different varieties of honey available in the shops today. We produce a large variety here in the British Isles, and we also import from other countries. Eucalpytus honey (imported from Australia) is my favourite: it has a strong flavour, and is renowned for its medical properties in the treatment of chest complaints. When I cannot get eucalpytus honey, I look for acacia honey, which is imported from Hungary and Romania. It is much milder than eucalyptus honey.

Natural, untreated honey is a nutritious, healthy food, possessing valuable medicinal properties as well as unequalled subtleties of flavour. When honey is heated, trace elements are destroyed. Liquid honeys are grouped into three colour grades – light, medium and dark. The lighter grades are usually derived from clovers, limes, acacias, brassicas, willow, herbs, sage and eucalyptus. The flavour tends to be delicate and subtle.

Medium honey sources are maple, sycamore, apples, plums, cherries, soft fruit, dandelions, Michaelmas daisies, and many more. They have a richer flavour, are thicker and granulate more coarsely.

Darker honey comes from chestnuts, blackberries, buckwheat and bushy plants. The flavour is quite strong and the granulation is more coarse than fine. Sometimes, the honey can be a mixture, which accounts for a variation of colour and flavour. The finest flavoured honey is taken straight off the hive in the comb, and eaten still warm from the bees.

I have brought up eight children and for thirty years I have treated coughs, colds, sore throats and chest complaints frequently. I learned never to be without honey in the house. For chest complaints, bronchitis, coughs and colds, my honey and onion cough mixture has never failed. I never went to the chemist for a cough medicine, I made my own.

Honey and onion cough medicine

Take 450 g/1 lb of liquid honey – eucalyptus if possible – and one empty honey jar, then slice finely one large Spanish onion. Put half the sliced onion into the empty jar, add half the liquid honey from the full jar and put the remainder of the sliced onion into the remaining liquid honey. Cover both jars and leave overnight, making sure the honey and onion in each jar is well mixed by turning the jars upside down from time to time. By the morning, the onion juice will have been extracted and mixed with the honey. The shrivelled onion can now be strained, and the honey and onion juice used as a most beneficial cough mixture. The honey is full of the B-vitamins which treat the nerves and produce a calming sleep; the onion is a natural antibiotic, killing any offending viruses. The mixture never fails, and is a wonderful energizing food.

Honey for asthma is unbeatable. My youngest daughter suffered from chest and lung trouble for many years. When she was four years old, I had seen her fight for breath. When I read Dr Jarvis's book *Folk Medicine*. I found he advocated sucking a honeycomb at the onset of an asthma attack. I took his advice and it worked miracles for my daughter. Because of the presence of B vitamins in the honey, it has a wonderful, instant calming effect on the nerves. In a few minutes my young daughter would settle and go to sleep.

I also used to take honey to calm my own nerves when I was taking driving lessons. I was then 40 years old, and going through a very severe menopause. I had already had a hysterectomy and the resultant hot flushes were pretty horrendous. HRT was not available in those days (even if it had been, I would not have taken it, particularly if I had known what I now know of the possible side-effects for some women). A driving lesson was a dreadful experience for me. I would sit in the car beside my very patient instructor and get a severe hot flush – until I used the honey treatment. About an hour before my driving lesson I started to take two teaspoons of honey. My nerves settled down, the hot flushes eased up and at my fourth attempt, I passed my test! I think I would have given up long before had it not been for the honey.

Sore throats were a common occurrence in our house: cider vinegar and honey were the antidote. I dissolved two teaspoons of honey in 300 ml/half a pint of hot water (not boiling), and added to this two teaspoons of cider vinegar. The sufferer sipped the mixture and then gargled with it two to three times a day. The cider vinegar killed the virus that was causing the sore throat, and the honey had a wonderful calming effect on the child, who soon slept peacefully. The doctor's visits to our family were few and far between.

Honey has proved excellent in the healing of wounds – I have even heard that honey is being used in some hospitals now to aid healing. Honey is also excellent in breathlessness, especially that related to emotional stress. As in asthma, it has a very calming effect on the nerves. Two teaspoons of honey straight from the honey-pot can work wonders (sucking a honeycomb produces the same effect).

Honey for hayfever

The efficacy of honey for hayfever was brought to a wide readership in the book *Folk Medicine* by Dr C. Jarvis, first published in 1958. He recommended chewing one teaspoonful of honeycomb three times a day, starting at least four months before the hayfever season begins. He also drew attention to the observation that honey cappings (the waxy coating made by the bees), being richer in pollen, were more effective. It is best if the honey taken is produced within a 15 km (ten-mile) radius of the sufferer. Local honey has a better chance of dealing with local pollens.

Honey for ulcers

For years, standard ulcer treatment has centred around counteracting acid secretion which causes indigestion, acid reflux, heartburn etc., but recent research has found that most gastric ulcers are caused by an infection of the *helicobacter pylori* bacteria, which weakens the protective lining of the stomach and intestines. Tests have shown that the growth of this bacteria is completely prevented by honey.

When a patient takes an antacid, it neutralizes the acid in the stomach, but in so doing, the stomach has to produce more acid to enable the digestive enzymes to work. Antacids do not treat the underlying problem – and they bring their own set of side-effects. In my opinion, it would be so much better to strengthen the mucous lining of the stomach with a daily dose of honey, which would prevent any invasion of the offending bacteria. This advice does not apply to diabetics, who must regulate their sugar intake.

Honey has the advantage of being absorbed relatively slowly when used as a sweetener in the diet. But make sure that the honey you buy is labelled 'raw' or 'unheated'.

If you have a yeast problem (*candidiasis*) you must not take honey until the condition is well under control. The yeast in the honey could aggravate the condition.

Honey for hyperactive children has also had remarkable results – possibly because of its calming effects on the nerves.

At my clinic, we have various alternatives to the honey and molasses in our treatments – but we realize that without cider vinegar we would get nowhere. I have never known anybody to reject it completely.

5

Case-notes from the clinic

Before patients are treated at our clinic, they have to fill in a detailed questionnaire, answering many questions about their health – i.e. past history, medication, current symptoms, and any other relevant information. We never treat children without seeing them and doing urine tests for the pH balance, blood, protein, nitrates, leukocytes, glucose, etc. We also test for zinc deficiency, blood pressure and take pulse-readings.

People who suffer only from arthritis can normally be advised from a distance – we have patients in many parts of the world. If, when reading a person's answers to the questionnaire, we find that they are taking a variety of drugs, we sometimes ask them to contact their doctor for urine tests, anaemia and thyroid tests, and furnish us with the results, so that we may treat them correctly if they cannot come to the clinic.

It is my sincere belief that all human beings have the right to live the best life they can and to choose whatever method they think best to gain good health and freedom from pain. It is our right to choose between conventional medicine, which deals with symptoms of disease, and natural methods, which aim to improve the immune system with high-quality nutrition.

Drugs prescribed by doctors (especially steroids) suppress the immune system. This I cannot understand. Without a healthy immune system we have no chance of attaining a long life and the happiness of which we all dream. We have many systems in our bodies (e.g. the digestive system, the circulatory system, the glandular system, the reproductive system, the nervous system and the immune system). None of these systems can function properly by themselves. They are all dependant on each other. If one is not working properly, all the others are incomplete and show signs of ill-health.

Research in recent years has found that we should eat more fruits, vegetables, grains and seeds for a healthy, long and active life. It saddens me that a lot of my patients have been told by their doctor that diet has nothing to do with their arthritis. On the contrary: I have found for years that diet has everything to do with all illnesses. It is my firm belief that arthritis, cancer, heart-trouble, diabetes, and many more illnesses, are directly related to the unnatural food that we are now living on. Our apples are sprayed with chemicals to make them bigger and look better, as are all our fruits and vegetables. These chemicals have ruined the nutritional value, so fruits and vegetables which once offered nourishment now do so no more. Sprays and chemical fertilizers not only add extra, harmful, ingredients, but they also destroy the nutritional value of the crops. The soil is a complex of inorganic and organic mineral complexes. Adding mineral or chemical fertilizer to the soil, of whatever quality, will tend to upset this delicate balance. The result could be that vitamin, mineral, amino acid and trace element uptake by the plants could be depressed, affecting the nutritional quality of the produce. Chemical pesticides, fungicides and herbicides are also used, and these too are taken up by crops. These contaminants are foreign to the body and can accumulate therein. Most cannot be removed by washing the fruit or vegetable.

The old adage 'An apple a day keeps the doctor away', is no longer true. Doctors' surgeries are full of people with all sorts of diseases: the quality of life has deteriorated to an all-time low.

It is time we stopped interfering with nature. People would be much healthier if they were to eat only organically grown fruits and vegetables, and to take responsibility for improving the conditions of life. More and more people these days are looking for ways to get fit and healthy.

I speak from personal experience. As I have already related, I developed rheumatoid arthritis at the age of 21. The pains in every joint of my body were excruciating. I was in constant pain, a nagging ache, with intermittent flare-ups, until eventually, 16 years on, I could not perform the simplest task without pain. I had backache, my feet were swollen and painful as were my hands and my knees. My jaws were locked and I could not chew my food. I was underweight and my nerves had gone to pieces. My whole body was so sore that I could not bear the dog to brush against me.

Looking back on all this, I associate it with the excess of dairy foods I had as a child. When I was young I was very underweight, and prone to infections. My mother fed me on the fat of the land. My father had a small farm; we kept our own cows, killed all our own pigs and grew our own vegetables. I never liked vegetables of any sort, but my mother insisted that I had plenty of milk straight from the cows. I always got the top of the milk, i.e. the cream. I loved it and my mother felt that it made up for the food I did not have because of my 'delicate stomach'. But I now feel that my diet in those days contributed in a very big way to my rheumatic condition later.

When I read Dr Jarvis' book, I began to understand the cause of my arthritis. I began to take cider vinegar, and my nursing training helped me a lot in changing to an acid-free diet – the same diet that is so beneficial to my patients today.

The combined regime of cider vinegar and an acid-free diet became a habit. My arthritis subsided, and gradually I got rid of it. I realized that, because my diet had for many years lacked essential vitamins and minerals, I had to replace these in any way I could; so I ate plenty of salads, non-citrus fruits, and grated raw vegetables. My heart returned to normal, and I became a healthy woman at the age of 37 years, having suffered for 16 years with crippling arthritis. I give thanks to God and Dr Jarvis for putting me on the right road and showing me the way ahead. I am now 71 years old, and to date I have not had a return of the arthritis. I do not keep strictly to the regime now, but I do take my own prescribed vitamins and minerals and a cider vinegar drink daily. This keeps me free.

When my patients are clear of their arthritis, I treat them as I do myself. They return to a normal diet, having a glass of wine if they wish and partaking of various other, previously forbidden, foods, but always taking their cider vinegar and a reduced vitamin and mineral programme. Some patients overdo their new-found freedom, and the acids in their bodies start to build up again. They know what to do. They go back to the old regime of diet, vitamins, minerals and cider vinegar three times daily. Soon they are clear of acids again.

It is wonderful for me to know that, through my suffering all those years ago, I can bring comfort and health to so many throughout the world today. We treat people in many parts of the world. A lot are suffering from the side-effects of drugs – the anti-inflammatory drugs or steroids. I give thanks to God for the day I got the idea of opening a clinic and writing my books. The benefits to me cannot be measured in pounds, shillings and pence, but in the smiles of gratitude on people's faces. Very few people fail to derive benefit from our treatment. Some take a long time to get good results; others improve relatively quickly.

The following are a selection of case histories from the clinic. All the patients have been on cider vinegar, plus different nutritional programmes according to their individual needs. All, too, have been on our low-fat acid-free diet.

Mrs S. wrote to us in February 1995, having had problems for about a year:

I began to wake up in the morning very stiff, and walking down the stairs was painful to the knees. Turning on the tap and lighting the kettle hurt my hands. After about three weeks things had got no better, and I visited my doctor who arranged blood tests. When I returned to see her, I had worsened. She said that the results showed an under-active thyroid gland and that the rheumatoid arthritis tests were positive. She wrote to the hospital to get me an appointment with the rheumatologist, which came through for the end of November – some time off. By now it was taking me until lunch-time to get fully mobile, and by evening all the aches and stiffness returned. My mother then gave me your book *Curing Arthritis the Drug-Free Way* – a friend of hers had lent it to her. I read it and decided to give the treatment a try. Within three weeks of starting the programme I felt better in myself generally. Gradually the morning stiffness grew less, and I was able to lift my arms above my head. After three months I started to play badminton again. The pain and stiffness was confined to only a few remaining places – in my feet, hands and elbows. It took about another three months or so for all symptoms to disappear. When I went for my last appointment to the hospital, I told them I was better. I know that your regime cured me, but the doctor was not impressed. However, I am continuing with the cider vinegar treatment, diet and supplements because I know it is the wisest thing to do.

Mrs S. is now clear of arthritis. She has got on extremely well in a very short time, mainly because she would not take any drugs for her arthritis. She never visited our clinic. She was quite prepared to come for a consultation, but, on processing the questionnaire she had completed, we felt that there was no need for an appointment. We were quite right. We assumed her immune system was low, so we treated her with zinc so that she would not feel her pain so intensely. (Approximately 90 per cent of the patients who apply to us for treatment are low in zinc.) She was also anaemic; we gave her extra iron and vitamin C to help the body absorb it. Taking iron alone, without vitamin C, is a dangerous practice. If the iron is not absorbed into the blood-stream it can settle in the liver and result in liver-poisoning.

Mrs S. was willing to help any other patients, so we introduced her to Mrs C., who has now started our treatment. We hope that Mrs C. will achieve similar results.

Mrs F. applied to us for treatment in May 1993. She was a patient from that date, taking all our treatments: vitamins, minerals, protein – and cider vinegar, honey and molasses. She is now free of suffering. Her last letter to us goes like this:

My symptoms were different from those of the general run of arthritis sufferers. My joints were not swollen, nor were my limbs twisted. I did have severe inflammation in my muscles and tissues. I had the sensation of being severely scalded, especially the muscles between my shoulder-blades, but in fact everywhere. When it was bad, even my eyelids, tongue and scalp were affected, giving acute pain and weakness, total misery. No one could diagnose what was wrong with me; a Harley Street rheumatologist put me on an antidepressant. I didn't in fact take the drugs, so I was left to suffer.

A friend told me about the Margaret Hills treatment, and gave me the book *Curing Arthritis the Drug-Free Way*. I started the treatment in April 1993 and I am now free from this awful malady. I did have to persevere. I did have flare-ups, but it has all been worthwhile. Thank you again for your help; to have the hand of hope stretched out in such circumstances is indescribable.

Mrs F. continued with our cider vinegar, honey, molasses, acid-free diet, with vitamins, minerals and proteins from May 1993 until November 1995. As she says, she is free from her malady but will continue with a reduced programme for the future, but she can now face the future with hope and thanks in her heart.

Mrs H. applied to us for treatment in December 1993. When she filled in our questionnaire she wrote: 'In the last three weeks the pain in my neck is worse, it is in my shoulders too with dreadful pain going down my right arm to my wrist'. She was in a lot of pain, and was not sleeping well; she also lacked calcium. She was taking a drug to stimulate her underactive thyroid; she was overweight and she was also on HRT. She had already started to take the cider vinegar, honey and molasses. She did not attend the clinic: we treated her by post and gave her advice and encouragement by telephone. It took her two years to clear herself of arthritis. In December 1995 she wrote to us:

I started your treatment two years ago, at which time I was in considerable pain in my feet, knees, wrists, thumb-joints and particularly in my shoulders. For the first two months of treatment I was unable to move my arms properly. Gradually, the pain disappeared from all joints except my shoulders, which continued to be painful. But as time went on the flare-ups lessened and eventually they lasted only two days.

The pain in my arm-muscles was the last to clear up, and at one time I felt that it was never going to improve. But I awoke one morning and found that I was completely free of pain. It was a wonderful feeling, and I could not quite believe that it was going to last. However, after being totally free of pain for three months, I am feeling absolutely great! I am so grateful that I discovered your treatment – it has certainly changed my life.

Some people work solely from the treatment prescribed in my first book *Curing Arthritis the Drug-Free Way*. This is fine if they are taking no drugs for arthritis, and if they have no complications. We do not even know that they are doing it until we get a letter such as the following one, which arrived in August 1993:

I am writing just to say that I suffered with rheumatoid arthritis for nearly two years. It started after being away on holiday in Cyprus. When I came back, one of my knees had doubled in size and I was getting horrific pains in my legs. I used to cry with pain.

My doctor sent me to see a specialist, as by then it had moved to my wrists and I did not know what to do because of all the pain I was getting. I could not even write a note for my daughter for school, because it looked as if a 5-year-old had written it. I was given pain-killers but even then I was still in pain; I was also given splints to wear on my hands at night and splints for the day. I honestly thought I would be on tablets for the rest of my life. But then a friend bought me a book called *Curing Arthritis the Drug-Free Way*.

I have been following the treatment advised in this book, and have been discharged from the hospital and now suffer no pain at all. I am just writing this in the hope that it will give someone, somewhere, faith in what you say.

Such letters arrive frequently at the clinic. I feel humble and privileged to know that the words I write are doing so much good to so many people.

In January 1992, a 12-year-old girl arrived at the clinic with her parents. She had been diagnosed with arthritis the previous June. She was very underweight. She had pericarditis (inflammation of the heart muscle), which frequently occurs in cases of rheumatoid arthritis. I believe that the virus that causes arthritis is streptococcus, and that pericarditis occurs when this virus attacks the heart. I have personal experience of this: when I had rheumatoid arthritis my heart became very badly enlarged. It was very comforting for the child's parents to know that my heart recovered completely and that, nearly 50 years on, I have not had a return of the virus. The girl had a very high temperature and could not sleep at night. I advised her parents to ask her GP for a test for anaemia as well as thyroid and liver-function tests. She was on various drugs, which I felt were causing the very high temperatures. I advised her to discontinue the drugs – which she did.

Her zinc test showed a very low immune system, so I gave her a zinc supplement, as well as prescribing the vitamins, minerals and proteins which I felt she needed. I also prescribed cider vinegar which, in my estimation, was the most important ingredient in her treatment. This was to kill the virus that was playing havoc with her whole body, ruining her life and that of her parents. I gave her a strong natural pain-blocker called DLPA to help her to discontinue the drugs. I also prescribed plenty of honey and black cane molasses. The amounts were all suitable for a very poor digestion (and for a child of her age).

I also advised her parents to keep in touch with her GP and the hospital. Blood tests and X-rays are invaluable to me in the treatment of my patients.

When she arrived for her second appointment, two months later, she had gone through very severe flare-ups; her knees were still swollen, but the heart problem had settled down. Great news! I knew the cider vinegar was doing its job in removing the uric acid from the body which had been nourishing the virus responsible for her trouble.

She had been to the hospital and had her liver-function tested, along with tests for anaemia and thyroid. All these tests showed that things were normal – I was pleased there was no need to worry about those areas. I did not change her treatment, but she had discontinued her drugs and was sleeping better. Three months later, she had started to put on weight and looked so much better.

By June 1993 she had put on a stone in weight and was doing very well. In June 1994, she came for her last appointment. She was now quite clear of arthritis. In the meantime I had received the following letter from her parents:

Please find enclosed two photographs of Fiona. One when she was ill with juvenile arthritis and one after 18 months of your treatment. My wife and I are over the moon with the progress she has made and so is her paediatrician – he discharged her on her last visit. He was amazed at the way she had progressed, and commented that, whatever your clinic is giving her, it is doing nothing but good and should have all the credit. The paediatrician sent her for more blood tests and told us if we do not hear from him in two weeks everything is OK. That was four months ago, and we still have not heard from him. Thank God, and thank you very much for all you have done. I shudder to think what would have been the outcome if we had kept her on the drugs. I know drugs can only bring false hope and misery, with more complications and side-effects along with continuity of arthritis.

She is now in excellent health and has become very friendly with a patient of mine in Northern Ireland, encouraging her along the way – and in fact is willing to talk to anyone who is in trouble with arthritis. She still takes her cider vinegar and a reduced programme of vitamins and minerals to keep the acids at bay.

Mrs G. joined us in November 1986. When she filled in the questionnaire, she said she suffered from migraine occasionally, also cramp in her legs, pins and needles and pain. She was 61 years old. She did not want to start taking drugs. She had read my book, *Curing Arthritis the Drug-Free Way*, and said that my approach to the problem of arthritis appealed to her. She had been diagnosed with arthritis three weeks previously. She took our basic treatment by post for two years until she was completely clear. She still follows our treatment and advice to the present day, and she is still completely free of any symptoms of arthritis. She wrote me the following letter in February 1989:

The success of the Margaret Hills treatment for rheumatism and arthritis was proved to me when I visited my oculist.

Some two years ago I went to him to renew my spectacles. He looked at the old pair I was using and remarked, 'Have you rheumatism?' I replied, 'It's funny you should say that, because my right knee is painful and now the left one is starting to pain me too.'

Shortly afterwards I started the Margaret Hills treatment regularly, with excellent results. When the time came to return to my oculist, he again looked at the frames and said, 'you no longer have rheumatism'. My reply was, 'How do you know that?' He answered that, on the previous frames, the gold under the ear-pieces was very discoloured – due, he said, to the acid on the skin working under the plastic covering and causing the metal to become very stained. My new frames – which I had been using while I was using the cider vinegar treatment – were not marked at all, and neither did I have any more pain.

What an interesting discovery!

We do get reports from our patients of various unexpected findings. For instance, one patient of ours, in her 60s, had practically white hair when she started our treatment four years ago. On her last visit she showed me that her hair had gone back to her natural brown colour, completely naturally. She was delighted – she did not like her grey hair anyway.

Another patient reportrd that his hair was growing again. Yet another said that his prostate gland had been completely healed through the treatment. It is wonderful for us to hear of these beneficial side-effects. I can only assume that these various symptoms (hair-loss, prostate trouble and greying hair) had been caused by lack of proper nutrition. When the body was properly nourished, the conditions reverted to normal.

I could fill many books with the positive results of our treatment – but there is no room. However, I do feel that the following one is interesting. In April 1988 we received the following letter:

My husband, Geoff, who is just 49, has recently been diagnosed as having rheumatoid arthritis. Wanting to know as much about this condition as possible, I bought your book. We were greatly encouraged by what we read, and embarked upon your regime straight away. We have both adopted a positive frame of mind and are determined to cure this disease.

I am alarmed at how rapidly this illness is affecting my husband. He appears to have become an old man in a matter of weeks, and is sometimes so uncomfortable with so much pain. He obviously has to continue with his job as best he can (he is an estate agent). We are expecting a new baby next month; we also have a handicapped child, so I am sure you must understand how important it is for him to get better.

At the moment he takes two anti-inflammatory tablets a day and co-proxamol [an analgesic], approximately six in 24 hours. He has also been prescribed Sulphasalazine [another anti-inflammatory drug] but has not started on these. Thank you so much for the help you have already given us through your book.

Later that month, Mr F. attended our clinic for a consultation. He had great trouble in walking, and could not go up or down stairs without severe pain. His hands were swollen and painful, and it was getting impossible for him to drive his car. Getting in and out of the bath was a real problem.

I did the usual tests, prescribed a good intake of cider vinegar and the necessary nutrition to bring about good health. He had been seeing the consultant at the hospital and his Erythrocyte

Sedimentation Rate, or ESR, which shows the level of inflammation in the body, as measured by a blood test, was 80.

He returned to the clinic two months later. He was getting severe flare-ups. But by September – just six months after starting our treatment – he was feeling very happy, still taking his cider vinegar and all other prescribed nutrients. In April 1989 he came for his last appointment. His consultant had discharged him and was very surprised at his progress.

He showed me a letter he received from his consultant which read: 'I am sure you will be delighted to know that your ESR test result is now 3, having been 80. Perhaps I should give up conventional medicine and take cider vinegar for the rest of my life.'

Glossary of terms

Candida
Genus of yeast like fungi.

Candida albicans
Species of the candida genus, common in the mouth, throat, vagina, intestinal tract and skin; may cause infection under certain conditions.

Candidiasis
Infection with fungus of the genus candida.

Crepitus
Crunching and creaking of the joints due to wearing away of synovial membranes.

E.S.R.
Erythrocyte Sedimentation Rate; the level of inflammation in the body.

Helicobacter pylori
Bacteria which weakens the protective lining of the stomach and intestines; growth of this bacteria is prevented by eating honey.

Hypertension
Abnormally high blood pressure.

Hypotension
Abnormally low blood pressure.

Migraine
Severe headache, typified by pain on one side of the head, disturbed vision and nausea.

Oedema
Swollen state of body tissues.

Osteoporosis
Weakness of the bones.

Pericarditis
Inflammation of the heart muscle.

Phlebitis
Inflammation of varicose veins.

Quinsy
Abcess forming around the tonsils.

Thrush
Disease associated with white spots on the mucous membranes of the mouth, caused by *candida albicans*, colloquial term for candidiasis of the vagina (cardidal vaginitis).

Toxaemia
Blood poisoning.

Index

Recipes